GERMANS
IN
Milwaukee

GERMANS

IN

Milwaukee

A NEIGHBORHOOD HISTORY

....

Jill Florence Lackey & Rick Petrie

THE
History
PRESS

Published by The History Press
Charleston, SC
www.historypress.com

First published 2021

Manufactured in the United States

ISBN 9781467147286

Library of Congress Control Number: 2020951673

Dedicated to the more than 1,200 Milwaukee informants who were interviewed in Urban Anthropology's ethnic and neighborhood studies, making this and other works possible.

Contents

Acknowledgements   9
Introduction   11

PART 1: REMAINS OF EARLIEST GERMAN SETTLEMENTS IN MILWAUKEE
NEIGHBORHOODS
  1. The "Old Lutherans"   17
  2. Early Catholics from Cologne   22
  3. Pennsylvania Dutch from Pennsylvania   27
  4. Jews from German-speaking Nations   33
  5. Forty-Eighters from German-speaking Nations   39
  6. The Pomeranian Germans of Jones Island   43
  7. Germans from Russia in Old North Milwaukee   50
  8. Donauschwaben from the Danube Region   54

PART 2: GERMAN PLACE NAMES IN MILWAUKEE NEIGHBORHOODS
  9. Neighborhoods   61
  10. Street Names   65

PART 3: REMAINS OF GERMAN COMMERCE IN MILWAUKEE NEIGHBORHOODS
  11. Shopping Hubs   75
  12. Other Retail   85
  13. Breweries   89
  14. Machine Shops   102

CONTENTS

15. Tanneries   108
16. Eats and Greets   116

PART 4: REMAINS OF GERMAN INSTITUTIONS IN MILWAUKEE NEIGHBORHOODS
17. Religion   127
18. Schools   132
19. Healthcare   139

PART 5: REMAINS OF GERMAN WAYS OF LIFE IN MILWAUKEE NEIGHBORHOODS
20. Social/Recreational   145
21. Arts/Cultural   151
22. Politics   156

PART 6: GERMAN FOOTPRINTS ON THE PHYSICAL TERRAIN IN MILWAUKEE NEIGHBORHOODS
23. Architecture   161
24. Landscape   168
25. Urban Renewal   174

PART 7: EFFORTS TO REMOVE GERMAN FOOTPRINTS FROM MILWAUKEE NEIGHBORHOODS
26. World War I   185
27. World War II   190

PART 8: RESTORING MILWAUKEE'S GERMAN ESSENCE
28. Summarizing the Footprints   195
29. Ways Milwaukee Is Resurrecting Its Germanness   198

Notes   203
Bibliography   211
Index   219
About the Authors   224

ACKNOWLEDGEMENTS

*T*his book would not have been possible without the long list of anthropologists and anthropology interns who conducted observation and interviews in Urban Anthropology's twelve-year Milwaukee ethnic study and oral history of over one hundred Milwaukee neighborhoods. These individuals include: Elizabeth Albert, George Anachev, Jonathan Armstrong, Ericka Bailey, Amanda Balistreri, Jill Barganz, Ole Bassen, Erin Bilyeu, Laurel Bieschke, Abena Ivory Black, Crystal Blair, Jaime Bodden, Sarah Bradley, Ed Bremberger, Bethany Canales, Katelyn Cathcart, Annette Centenno, Gabrielle Charles, Isabella Clark, Havah Cohn-Mitchell, Shelby Lina Comeau, Stacey Cushenberry, Michelle Dekutowski, Katy Dineen, Helena Dulaney, Emily Eiseman, Alejandra Estrin, Kathrin Fiedler, Julia Field, Bix Firer, Laura Finley, Jesse Fujinaka, Erinn Brittney Gedemer, Chrissy Haikel, Carolyn Hall, Amy Hilgendorf, Susan Hill, Scott Hamann, Edith Hammond, Meghan Houlehen, Whitney Johnson, Tony Johnson, Lynn Johnston, Jessica Kegel, Nora Klein, Nkosi Knight, Beth Krueger, Joe Kubisiak, Ayn Lee, Martha Leuthner, Imani London, Erin Malcolm, Andreana Martin, Melissa Mason, Jeremy Mattson, Cloe McCabe, Aimee McGinty, Petra Moran, Jamie Merkel, Denise Meyer, Rebecca Mueller, Sarah Munson, Joy Irene Neilson, Brenda Nemetz, Martha Novotny, Kim Osborn, Danielle Paswaters, Rita Petri, Ashley Piatak, Brooke Phelps, Troy Potter, Dulce Ramos, Nicole Rice, Sara Rich, Anna Reidy, Paul Rivas, Mary Roffers, Anastacia Scott, Jason Scott, Kathrin Schmid, AnnMarie Seiser, Lily Shapiro, Megan Sara Sharpless, Lisa Spencer, Amy Svinicki, Tracey

ACKNOWLEDGEMENTS

Tessman, Mike Theis, Jeff Thomas, Rebecca Rae Torgerson, Alexandra Trumbull, Ciska Ulug, Chanel Updyke, Jenna Valoe, Tony Varono, Amanda Vilanueva, Lauren Christine Walls, Chris Weber, Ashley Widowski, Kelly Willis, Amanda Ybarra and Natalie Ann Zitnak.

Introduction

Perspectives of this Book: Neighborhood Physical Remains and Neighborhood Voices

It is not surprising that a wealth of literature is available on German hegemony in Milwaukee. In no other major American city did Germans achieve the degree of domination that they did in Wisconsin's largest urban center. This book will look at this presence from slightly different angles. First, it will focus on the physical remains left behind by the long Teutonic presence in the city—remains that can be seen in most of Milwaukee's nearly two hundred neighborhoods today. It will discuss the history and current function of the German-generated buildings, compounds, artifacts, statuary, physical remains and parklands.

Second, this book will offer an assessment of the German presence in the city from the ground level through the words of the city's residents. The authors direct a Milwaukee nonprofit organization, Urban Anthropology Inc. Since 2000, over 100 anthropologists and anthropology interns working with the nonprofit have participated in ethnic and neighborhood studies of the city. To date, rigorous observation has taken place in all of Milwaukee's neighborhoods, and over 1,200 Milwaukee informants have been interviewed about their city's history, culture, practices and policies, resulting in over fifteen thousand pages of oral history transcripts. Quotes from neighborhood and ethnic informants offer experiential perspectives and family history information on how the German presence remained stable or changed over time and how that presence is regarded today.

A Brief Overview of German Milwaukee: From Humble Settlements to the German Athens of America

The first major wave of Germans arrived in the area that would become Milwaukee in 1839. Others followed, all with their own reasons for leaving Europe and choosing to settle where they did. German informants from Urban Anthropology's twelve-year study of Milwaukee ethnic groups discussed the reasons their ancestors chose Wisconsin and Milwaukee.[1]

People just kept writing back that this was a nice place to come to, and so, they came. The very first arrived in Pennsylvania. That was in pre-Revolutionary days. Some of my ancestors went there first. As different waves started coming into the country, they discovered the Midwest. So, they came in large numbers here [Milwaukee], southern Ohio, Missouri, and then a large number went to Texas in the 1840s.

Wisconsin was so similar to their homeland. The land. Later, in Milwaukee, it was the industries, the breweries. German culture. For my great-great-grandfather, it was the breweries.

The area was right, and the timing was perfect. Germans arrived in great numbers just as Milwaukee's urban center was forming. While some came with wealth and others arrived with little more than a change of clothes, the Teutonic immigrants brought ambition of varying dimensions with them. Some began their paths to success by organizing commercial and institutional microorganisms, living frugally and gradually building up the enterprises over multiple generations. Others worked their way into powerful families. The record shows numerous examples of new immigrant laborers marrying daughters, sisters, nieces and widows of industrial and commercial bosses and then leading their old firms to new heights. And the German entrepreneurs and their families did not direct from boardrooms. They were more likely to be the first to arrive in the morning—no matter how hefty the enterprises had grown—and the last to go home, always keeping their eyes and hands on every subunit within their realm.

Just decades after the arrival of the first settlers, new settlers developed infrastructure, faith communities, educational institutions, musical societies, playhouses, athletic clubs, freedom-of-thought organizations, industries, beer gardens and breweries—all with a particular German piquancy. At the time, there were more German-language newspapers in Milwaukee than English ones. In time, locals and visitors alike began to compare Milwaukee's architecture, shops, theaters and educational elements to those of Athens in Ancient Greece. Milwaukee became known as *das Deutsche Athen von Amerika* or "the German Athens of America."

While it was interrupted during the two world wars, German cultural domination of Milwaukee continued into the mid-twentieth century. As the city aged, many Germans began a gradual migration into Milwaukee's suburbs, and the age of Teutonic hegemony came to an understated end. This book will concentrate on what is left of this once-strong presence and how it manifested and continues to manifest itself in specific Milwaukee neighborhoods today.

PART 1

Remains of Earliest German Settlements in Milwaukee Neighborhoods

1

THE "OLD LUTHERANS"

*T*he first major wave of German settlers in the area that would become Milwaukee were known as the "Old Lutherans." The majority of these settlers were activists from Brandenburg and Pomerania who were fleeing royal attempts to merge the Evangelical Lutheran and Reformed Protestant denominations into a Prussian state church. Having resources to make the move, some of the immigrants settled on land in today's Mequon, Wisconsin, and organized the hamlet of Freistadt, or "Free Town."

A few miles south in the area that would become Milwaukee, land developers Byron Kilbourn and Solomon Juneau were competing for settlers. In 1839, Kilbourn gave land to one of the newly arrived Old Lutherans. He and other members of his community ended up settling in an area near Third Street and Chestnut in today's Westown neighborhood.[2] They quickly erected a half-timber building as a church.

As the community grew, the Old Lutherans sought space for a cemetery. They began to chart out land just west of their settlement in today's King Park neighborhood, which would ultimately become known as the Second Ward, German Protestant or the Gruenhagen Cemetery.[3] This cemetery would attract considerable local attention in 2015.

THE GRUENHAGEN BROTHERS
AND THE BIRTH OF A CEMETERY

While they only had limited involvement in the development of the cemetery, the Gruenhagen brothers, Johann and Joachin, are often associated with it. The oldest brother, Johann, was born in 1800 in Pomerania. He came to the United States in 1836 with his wife, Friedericke Augusta (née Trieglaff), and their four children. By 1839, he'd settled on the land that had been given to his community by Byron Kilbourn. There, he was joined by his younger brother, Joachim, who'd been born in Pomerania in 1806. Joachim arrived with wife, Caroline Wilhelmina (née Bath), and their two children. Both families built homes on Third Street.

In 1848, Johann Gruenhagen purchased forty additional acres of land just west of his home—land whose titleship he apparently shared with Joachim. When Johann's third son, David Friedrich "Fritz," died in 1849, he buried him in that parcel of land. The following year, Joachim sold the land where Fritz was buried to William Ferdinand Otto, and the transaction resulted in the incorporation of the Second Ward Cemetery Association with trustees Joachim Luck, Benjamin Church and William Ferdinand Otto. The resultant cemetery was developed between Twelfth and Fourteenth Streets on Chestnut (today's West Juneau Avenue).

The sale of the land provided the Gruenhagen brothers with new opportunities. Neither remained in Milwaukee following that transaction. Almost immediately after the sale of the cemetery land, Joachim—apparently attracted by the rumors of California gold—left for San Francisco. The 1860 census lists him there as a miner. Two of his children died in California, and Joachim died there over a decade later.

Johann also left Milwaukee. By 1860, he and his family are recorded as living in Oshkosh, Wisconsin. There, Johann opened a store. He died in Oshkosh in 1881.

But what happened to the cemetery? A part of that story lies in the activities of William Ferdinand Otto.

WILLIAM FERDINAND OTTO
AND A CEMETERY FORGOTTEN

William Ferdinand Otto was born in Pomerania in 1822. He was a late addition to the Old Lutheran community, arriving in 1848 with his first wife,

Caroline, and their daughter, Emma. He apparently had ample resources. After purchasing the cemetery land from the Gruenhagens and becoming a trustee of the Second Ward Cemetery Association, he moved several blocks north to the Sixth Ward, where he built a home valued at $3,000 and maintained at least one servant. According to the 1860 U.S. Census, William Otto was then married to Wilhelmina. Caroline probably died sometime shortly after the birth of their son, Gustaf, in 1852 and was likely buried in the Second Ward Cemetery.

Following the births of their children Mary, Martha and Edward, the Ottos moved back to the Second Ward, where William Ferdinand may have continued his work with the cemetery, despite that fact that city ordinances prevented further burials there after 1861. In 1870, the property was auctioned, and four years later, the Common Council of the City of Milwaukee, resolving to extend Thirteenth Street through the former cemetery grounds, advised families to remove their dead.

However, it is not clear how completely the Old Lutheran community honored these decrees. After 1860, the Otto family was recorded as living at Twelfth Street and Chestnut, at the entrance of the cemetery. In fact, in the 1880 census, William Ferdinand Otto and his family are recorded as still living at that address, and his occupation is listed as "undertaker."

William Ferdinand and Wilhemina Otto eventually moved in with their son Edward's family on Seventh Street. William died sometime after 1910. At this point, the cemetery had become a talking point of the past—at least until 2015.

THE EXCAVATION AND A CEMETERY RESURRECTED

In 2013, the Cultural Resource Management of the University of Wisconsin–Milwaukee (UWM-CRM) was called to the site of the one-time Second Ward Cemetery after some bones were inadvertently disturbed during construction of a rain pavilion. The remainder of the excavation was monitored by UWM-CRM personnel.

But on July 19, 2015, while UWM-CRM staff was again on site, the Guest House of Milwaukee, a homeless shelter, was constructing an addition to this former Lot 3 land. As excavation began, human bones were encountered, and the process was halted. Given the history of the site, permission was requested and granted by the director of the Wisconsin Historical Society

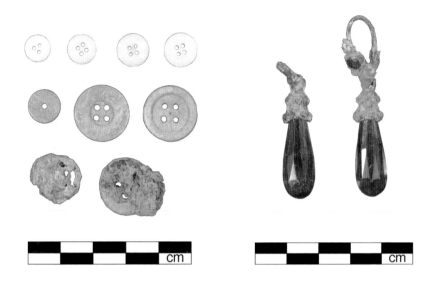

Buttons (*left*) and earrings (*right*) excavated from the Second Ward Cemetery. *University of Wisconsin–Milwaukee Cultural Resource Management.*

for UWM-CRM personnel to conduct a controlled excavation of the construction area and remove any burials they encountered.

The excavations took place from July to September 2015. The recovery included eighty individuals (fifty-two adults and twenty-eight juveniles) and personal and noncontemporary artifacts, such as evidence of previous disturbances. Personal effects of the individuals buried at the cemetery included earrings, belt buckles, coinage, rings and buttons.

Analysis of the individuals and their personal effects offered some information on the health and causes of death of those interred at the Old Lutherans' Second Ward Cemetery. While there was some indication of skeletal pathology or congenital abnormality among some individuals, most of the adult population had evidence of physical stress and age linked to their deaths, and most of the juveniles were affected by infection and nutritional deficiency—all conditions that could have been related to the pressure of the immigrant experience. Archaeologists continue to analyze the artifacts and remains to offer new insights on Milwaukee's earliest German experience. Approximately 4,138 graves still remain intact within the cemetery's boundaries.

THE LEGACY OF THE OLD LUTHERANS:
"WE SEE A RESURGENCE"

During Urban Anthropology's study of Milwaukee's ethnic groups, several German informants who were direct descendants of the Old Lutherans discussed the resurgence of ethnic identity in these early settlements and the stories and traditions that had been handed down over the generations from those in Milwaukee and, most particularly, those who made their home in Freistadt.

And one group of Pomeranians got together and sold all of their holdings that they had in Germany and converted it to gold and silver, and then they came over to the United States. They landed in New York, and while they were traveling over the seas from Pomerania to New York, there was one woman chosen each day to sit on that chest of gold and silver to make sure that no one took it away. It was always guarded. And they took the Erie Canal into the Great Lakes, St. Lawrence Seaway, and ended up here in Milwaukee. At that time—in 1843 to 1848—Milwaukee was a very poor area. They were dealing in script paper money. Script was good in Milwaukee, but it wasn't good in Waukesha, and it wasn't good in Chicago. So, they had to have gold and silver, so when the Pomeranians came over with this chest of gold and silver, they had to buy horses and wagons and farm implements, so it made Milwaukee wealthier than Chicago at that time. So, that's what kept the city floating, and that is, of course, Freistadt, and Freistadt means free city. So, they themselves came with that purpose in mind. Isn't that wonderful?

In Freistadt, you had people speaking Plattdeutsch until the middle of the 20th century. Even when you seemed to be losing a little of the culture, you got it back. We had forty kids that went to Germany to learn—I'd like to say relearn—Pomeranian folk dances....People are looking for that in their lives as we see a resurgence.

2.

EARLY CATHOLICS FROM COLOGNE

*I*n the early 1840s, a group of mainly Catholic German immigrants from the rural areas around the Rhine River and Cologne (*Köln* in German) acquired homesteads on heavily forested Wisconsin lands that had been ceded by the Potawatomi Natives. Their original settlement became a farming hamlet on Howell near today's College Avenue. They called their hamlet New Coeln (or New Köln). The region where they settled had just been designated the Town of Lake by the Territory of Wisconsin, and it would later be annexed to Milwaukee and become the neighborhood of New Coeln at the edge of Milwaukee Mitchell International Airport on the city's far south side.[4] By 1847, the hamlet had approximately fifty settlers and a new Catholic parish.

St. Stephen's Catholic Church: An Incredible Survival

Situated among the farm acres of the German immigrants was a privately owned log cabin that was originally used for celebrating mass once a month. Once settled, the landowners contributed logs for the construction of a formal church that was completed in 1847. By 1850, they had added a rectory and school. The community named its parish St. Stephen's Catholic Church after St. Stephen, the first martyr of Christianity. In 1884, the parishioners rebuilt the church.

St. Stephen's Church in 1912, after the rebuilding following the 1908 fire. A later version of the church still stands in Milwaukee's southern suburb of Oak Creek. *Milwaukee Archdiocese.*

But St. Stephen's Catholic Church would experience a long chain of tragedies. It burned down on May 13, 1908, was reconstructed and again burned down on January 1, 1926—this fire overcame both the church and the rectory. Yet again, the hardy German settlers voted to rebuild. The new church, with an altar and sanctuary carved from Slovenian white oak, survived another fire in 1979—this time, due to arson.

Despite its great persistence, St. Stephen's Catholic Church eventually moved. Over the years, it had become a more diverse metropolitan parish and found itself engulfed in airport expansion and competition from nearby churches. Under pressure from the archbishop to close, join another parish or rebuild in Oak Creek (a suburb just south of Milwaukee), the parishioners chose the latter. No longer a pillar of its original New Coeln community, the Oak Creek church broke ground in 2008—but again, not without misfortune. A month prior to its opening, lightning struck the bell tower. The church once again survived and was formally dedicated in November 2009.

But after returning to the early New Coeln neighborhood, the German settlers continued farming and did so well into the late twentieth century.

THE DEUSTERS, THE NEW COELN HOUSE AND HORSES WITH GOOD MEMORIES

The Deuster family played an important role in the New Coeln settlement. After emigrating from Blens, Rheinland, Preussen, Germany, in 1844, they arrived in the United States and purchased acreage in the Town of Lake. Among their neighbors were the Bower, Klein, Platt, Eppenech, Kebler and Lentz families. While most of the German settlers were Catholic, some, including the Kleins, were Lutherans. John Klein was an organizer of St. John's Evangelical Lutheran Church in 1850. Like St. Stephen's, this parish later moved to Milwaukee's southern suburb of Oak Creek.

The patriarch of the Deuster family was John Hubert Deuster, who was born in Germany in 1812. He married Anna Barbara Eppenech Deuster, and the couple had seven children. John Hubert Deuster was a key player in the founding of the first St. Stephen's Catholic Church. He not only contributed building logs, but he also donated a five-acre tract of his own land for its construction. Census records indicate that many of the Deusters worked as tailors as well as farmers.

The Deusters also played an important role in the development of another New Coeln institution. Originally called the New Cologne House, the Italianate-inspired saloon was built in the late 1840s. It originally functioned as a weighing station and inn for farmers traveling between Racine and Milwaukee Counties. Stories circulated that many Racine farmers, who imbibed too much beer in the saloon after selling their produce in Milwaukee, fell sound asleep in their horse-drawn wagons on the way home to their farms. Fortunately, as the tales go, the horses knew the routes of their sleeping masters and were able to deliver them safely home. Other stories circulated over the years that the inn had become a brothel, was haunted and served as a pharmacy for "quack medicine" on its second floor. (See a historic photograph of this building in the next section.)

The Coeln House underwent many name changes over the years, including the New Cologne House, New Coeln House, New Coeln Housdance Hall and Deuster's Saloon. Between the late 1860s and well into the twentieth century, the Deuster family ran the inn. Joseph Deuster, the son of John Hubert Deuster, maintained the establishment for decades. Born in Germany in 1835, he'd married Addie, had children and owned a farmhouse on Clinton Street (today's South First Street). U.S. Census records show him still managing the saloon as a widow in 1900, with several of his grown children remaining at home. His oldest son, Robert, took over the bar from him. Joseph Deuster died in 1914 and was buried at Holy Trinity Cemetery.

Today, the original saloon is still in operation in the New Coeln neighborhood at 5905 South Howell Avenue. Known as the Landmark 1850 Inn, it is Milwaukee's oldest functioning tavern.

DOGGED BUT DOOMED PERSEVERANCE

The New Coeln settlement was one of the most stable in Milwaukee's history. Among the German informants in Urban Anthropology's twelve-year study of Milwaukee's ethnic groups were several descendants of the original emigrants from the Cologne area. They described the unwavering nature of their ancestors and their community.

> *My great-grandmother spoke nothing but German.…She was dead before I was born, but my mom said she was an old German woman, and she refused to speak any English. She was born German, and she came over here, and she was going to speak German until the day she died.*

> *They came from Cologne, although they were farmers, so I doubt if they actually came from the city. They must have come from the outlying areas.…I believe it was my great-great-great-grandfather. He made the decision that everyone was going. So, there was no say in that with anybody else. He told everybody that was related to us that we're going to America. This is where we're going, and we're going to farm there. Essentially, everybody that we knew packed up and came over here and settled.…It had something to do with the lack of land* [in Germany], *and the rising prices, and that it was a lot cheaper over here.*

> *Well, up until my generation, they were all farmers. And they also raised pigeons.* [Interviewer: Pigeons? Is there money in that?] *No, they ate them. So, they raised a lot of pigeons for themselves and then they had like their own little garden plots where they'd get some of their stuff. But mostly, it was just farming. Corn. Corn, basically. And I guess recently now we've gone to more like a service-industry-type thing. Yeah, I guess like everyone else in the population. Actually, my sister's the first one not to be born on a farm. So, I still come from the farm.*

However, change was inevitable for the German community. In marched Milwaukee Mitchell International Airport and a myriad of highways. The drive for twentieth-century transportation systems in New Coeln transformed the German farmlands into runways for planes and wide bands of concrete highways for vehicles. As late as the 1970s, some descendants of the original German community remained on their land, including members of the Duester family. A *Milwaukee Journal* article in

1976 described their frustrations over exhaust fumes from the airport polluting their farmlands, brown rain and vibrations from the planes and traffic interfering with their sleep. Ultimately, most of the descendants of the original New Coeln community found new homes.

3.

PENNSYLVANIA DUTCH

FROM PENNSYLVANIA

*O*ver fifty neighborhoods on Milwaukee's northwest side were once encompassed by the Granville Township in Milwaukee County. The township extended from Hampton Avenue to the south, County Line Road to the north, 27th Street to the east and 124th Street to the west.

According to an 1877 article in the *Milwaukee Sentinel*, there were originally three small settlements in the Granville area. Beginning in 1835, the family of Jacob Brazelton and his eleven sons arrived. Next came Daniel R. Small and W.P. Woodward from Indiana. The third group of settlers, S.C. Enos and the Joseph R. Thomas family, arrived shortly after Small and Woodward.

Within a few years, new settlers emigrated from the town of Granville in Washington County, New York. The group included the Lake, Dutcher, Evert, Brown, Crippen and Norton families. They gave their new Wisconsin settlement the name of their former hometown in New York.

However, it was not these early arrivals who established the character of Granville Township. That function belonged to a wave of Pennsylvania "Dutch" (i.e., Germans) who arrived just a few years later from Pennsylvania. The Pennsylvania Dutch (*Pennsilfaanisch-Deitsche*) was a German-speaking cultural group, many of whom had emigrated from the Palatinate of the German Rhine during the seventeenth and eighteenth centuries. Families included in their Granville numbers were the Wambolds, Barndst, Prices, Bergstressers, Leisters, Scholls, Borses, Kleins, Martins, Hubers, Grolls, Hornings and Lewises. The Pennsylvania Dutch, under the guidance of Samuel Wambold, quickly formed the German Evangelical Lutheran and

Reformed Church (now known as Salem Evangelical Lutheran Church) in 1847 in today's Maple Tree neighborhood.[5]

THE WAMBOLDS

Samuel Wambold was the first individual to sign the church's charter constitution in 1847. Elected as the first elder, he was also chosen as master builder for the first log church.

Samuel Wambold was born in 1799 in Rockhill Township, Bucks, Pennsylvania. Sometime in the 1820s, Samuel married Elizabeth Kramer, who was born in 1801 in Francona, Montgomery, Pennsylvania. The couple moved back and forth from Bucks County to Montgomery County until 1847, when they joined other Pennsylvania Germans and migrated west to the Granville area. Over these migrations, they had eight children.

Samuel Wambold's death was the first recorded in Salem Church history. He died in 1849 at the age of fifty and was buried at West Granville Cemetery. His wife, Elizabeth, died in 1857 and was also buried at West Granville Cemetery. The cemetery was another creation of the Pennsylvania German settlers and was designated as a historic landmark in 1977.

FOUNDING OF WISCONSIN SYNOD

The original German Evangelical Lutheran and Reformed Church was built using logs and was dedicated in 1849. In December of the same year, Pastor Wilhelm Wrede called a meeting of local Lutheran ministers. Attending were Wrede, John Muehlhaeuser of Grace Lutheran Church in Milwaukee and John Weinmann of St. John Lutheran Church in Oak Grove. The three met in the Grace Church hall and formulated plans to organize a new church body—the First German Evangelical Lutheran Synod of Wisconsin. Muehlhaeuser was elected president, Weinmann secretary and Wrede treasurer.

The first synod convention took place at Salem Lutheran Church in Granville on May 26, 1850. Representatives of eighteen congregations attended and created a constitution. This event marked the founding of the Wisconsin Evangelical Lutheran Synod, a Lutheran denomination that has become an international church body. Thus, the Wisconsin Synod was born at Salem Lutheran Church in Granville.

The Salem Church in 1919, also known as the "Landmark Church." It still stands today at 6814 North 107th Street as a footprint of the early Pennsylvania Dutch settlers. *Salem Evangelical Lutheran Church.*

By 1861, the congregation had outgrown the log church and replaced it with Salem Lutheran Landmark Church, an excellent example of Italianate architecture. A school was added in the late 1800s. The new parish served the community well into the 1970s. The building still stands on North

107th Street and has been transformed into a museum of these early synod activities. Tours are available by appointment. The church was designated a City of Milwaukee Historic Site in 1992.

JOHANN HEINRICH SIEKER: SALEM CHURCH'S FIRST FULL-TIME PASTOR

Johann Heinrich Sieker was born in Baden, Germany, in 1839 and immigrated to the United States with his family as a child. Johann and his family settled in Newton, Wisconsin. Like his future congregants, Johann also had a Pennsylvania connection. He attended and graduated from Gettysburg Seminary in Gettysburg, Pennsylvania. In 1861, he received the call to the log cabin church, where he became the first pastor to come out of the newly organized Wisconsin Synod.

The same year, Johann received the call to Granville, where he married Julie Streissguth, who had been born in Germany in 1838. The couple would remain childless during their six years of service in Granville, but they oversaw the building of the later house of worship known as Salem Lutheran Landmark Church.

Johann and Julie left Granville for St. Paul, Minnesota in 1867 and served the Minnesota Synod until 1876. There, the couple had six children. The Siekers spent their last years of service in New York City, where Johann helped found the Concordia Collegiate Institute. Johann died in New York at the age of sixty-five in 1904.

DEVELOPMENT IN GRANVILLE

Interspersed with the Pennsylvania Dutch settlers in Granville Township were small communities of North American Natives, Irish and other Germans. The area was economically prosperous, likely due in part to the work ethic of the early residents. Remaining predominantly rural through the early half of the twentieth century, Granville was an important center for dairy and truck farming. Following World War II, industries began to open in Granville, and the area eventually became the most concentrated base of industrial employment in Wisconsin. Today it has industrial parks and scores of companies. Some of the early Germans left their footprints on industrial and commercial corridors in Granville.

THE SCHWISTERS OF THE MAPLE TREE NEIGHBORHOOD

Henry Schwister was born in Germany in 1875. He immigrated to the United States and Granville, where he married Clara Johnen from an old Granville farming family in 1902. He subsequently worked on her brother's farm.

By 1910, Clara and Henry were able to lease their own farm along today's Fond du Lac Avenue, although the property was not owned outright during Henry's lifetime. Henry died relatively early at the age of fifty-four, leaving the farm in the hands of his widow, Clara, and the couple's children. While most of the older children left school and continued working for the family business, Henry's son Henry J. ended up taking a job at an auto body factory. It may have been this experience that gave him the idea to open an auto dealership.

By 1940, Henry J. Schwister owned his own enterprise that would ultimately be known as Schwister Ford—becoming one of the largest Ford dealerships in the state of Wisconsin. The dealership was apparently built on or very near the family's original farmland. Henry J. married Marie Nellen, and the couple had four children. The family eventually opened a second Schwister Ford in Menomonee Falls and moved there. Henry J.'s son Eugene took over the Granville business on Fond du Lac from his father. Henry J. Schwister died in 1996 at the age of eighty-nine.

Henry J.'s brother, Edwin Schwister, assumed employment as a mechanic for Schwister Ford. He lived at 102nd and Fond du Lac, only a block from the dealership. Being perhaps as industrious as his brother, Edwin opened his own liquor store on his block—Eddie's Beer and Liquor. He died at the age of ninety-four in 2008.

ANNEXATION OF GRANVILLE

In the 1950s, the property owners and residents of Granville—who were overwhelmingly German—were offered a choice to consolidate with the city of Milwaukee. Needing services that Milwaukee could offer, including water from Lake Michigan, the majority of voters said yes to the referendum. By the 1960s, the western portion of Granville was annexed by Milwaukee, and parts of the eastern section consolidated with the village of Brown Deer. At the time and continuing to this day, Milwaukee became one of the few large cities in the United States to still have working farms within its boundaries.

In 2018 and 2019, Urban Anthropology Inc. conducted an oral history of the Granville (now Milwaukee) neighborhoods. Many of those who were interviewed reminisced over their rural upbringing.

When we weren't on a farm, my dad had a milk route. And I think, back then, he took the milk from farmers. I remember riding with him. We had two acres of land and a small garden. And eight kids. I was the oldest of eight....I knew a lot of kids in the neighborhood. And we hung around, played baseball, played sports. Kinda did things that most kids do. I remember one thing. My wife is astonished when I tell her this. To get around—of course, there was no public transportation or anything, and we couldn't drive or anything—it was pretty common to hitchhike.

I think that maybe the annexation by the city and the zoning changes that did come with that, I think that a lot of the land that was agricultural and not valued real highly became higher valued all of a sudden. That pushed farmers to sell their property, and that kind of encouraged the rapid development that took place.

4.

Jews from
German-speaking Nations

Unlike the German Lutherans and Catholics discussed earlier, the German Jews did not come to Milwaukee in organized religious groups. Bearing German surnames such as Adler, Weil and Heller, they arrived as individuals or small families from German-speaking states and the Austrian Empire beginning in the early 1840s. The immigrants quickly began establishing themselves in Milwaukee as shopkeepers and professionals. Within six years of the first arrival, Emanuel Shoyer opened a tailor shop; Joseph Schram followed with a grocery store; and a Jewish clothing manufacturer was established on Water Street. Lacking the legal restrictions they'd experienced in their homelands, the newly incorporated city of Milwaukee must have seemed like a deliverance.

However, religion was not ignored. In 1847, the German-speaking newcomers held their first Rosh Hashanah (Jewish New Year) service in the home of Henry Newhouse. Shortly afterward, they observed Yom Kippur (Day of Atonement) above the Pereles Grocery Store. The groundwork was being set to establish a formal congregation.

By 1849, the first Jewish birth in Milwaukee was recorded.

Emma Scheftels Herbst:
The First German Jew Born in Milwaukee

Emma Scheftels was born on September 16, 1849, to parents Henry and Barbara Scheftels, just a year after the couple had arrived in Milwaukee from the Austrian Empire. The couple and their child settled in a unit near Cedar Street (today's Kilbourn Avenue), just west of downtown, with Adolph Weil, another recent Jewish emigrant from the Austrian Empire. There, Henry and Barbara established a grocery and dry goods store.

At the age of eighteen, Emma married twenty-five-year-old Solomon C. Herbst, another German Jewish immigrant. Records suggest that Solomon may have arrived in Milwaukee alone. The 1860 U.S. Census indicates that, as a teenager, Solomon lived with another immigrant family, the Nathans, who owned a clothing store in Milwaukee's Historic Third Ward.[6] Solomon was employed as a clerk in the shop.

However, Solomon and Emma Herbst did not struggle long. While raising five children, they opened a wholesale liquor dealership. The enterprise must have been successful because they ended up purchasing a home on Nineteenth Street, where they employed three servants. They also took their children on a trip back to their German homelands in the 1880s.

The Herbst couple later moved to a home on Shepard Street on Milwaukee's Upper East Side, where they again employed several servants.[7] Emma died in 1910. She was buried at Greenwood Cemetery, where her parents were also interred.

CONGREGATION EMANU-EL B'NE JESHURUN: ONE FROM THE MANY

Following the formation of the Emanu-El Cemetery Association in 1848, 70 Jewish families came together to organize Congregation Imanu-Al in 1850, with Solomon Adler as president. Those who chose to worship in the Polish tradition as opposed to the German established Congregation Ahavath Emuno. Later, members of Ahavath Emuno who found they ended up preferring the German customs left to form a third congregation, Anshe Emeth. Three synagogues then served the small Jewish community of approximately 150 families. However, in 1852, on the suggestion of Isaac Mayer Wise, the founder of Reform Judaism, Ahabath Emuno and Imanu-Al consolidated as Congregation B'ne Jeshurun. Anshe Emeth joined them three years later.

But the unity did not last. In the early 1870s, thirty-five families elected to split off to Congregation Emanu-El. Reform Temple Emanu-El was built on Martin (now State Street). The two synagogues remained apart for fifty-eight years.

Reform Temple Emanu-El, which was built on Martin (today's State Street) and Broadway in 1872. Photograph taken circa 1890. *Jewish Museum Milwaukee.*

The congregation of Emanu-El B'ne Jeshurun, which was built on East Kenwood Boulevard in the 1920s. Photograph taken circa 1955. *Jewish Museum Milwaukee.*

By the 1920s, Emanu-El was in need of larger facilities and began erecting a new building at 2419 East Kenwood Boulevard in the Upper East Side neighborhood.[8] In the meantime, B'ne Jeshurun's structure was also becoming obsolete. After much deliberation, the two congregations agreed to share the building on Kenwood. Congregation Emanu-El B'ne Jeshurun emerged.

The new congregation remained stable at that location for over seventy years, and its rabbis became major leaders in the Milwaukee community. But seeing its Reform congregants moving in large numbers to Milwaukee's northern suburbs and facing other issues, it moved to the Joseph and Vera Zilber campus in the suburb of River Hills in 2000.

However, the footprint of the sometimes embattled but always relevant congregation of German Jewish origins remains intact. Today, the building on Kenwood Boulevard is part of the University of Wisconsin-Milwaukee—now, the Helene Zelazo Center for the Performing Arts.

MILWAUKEE'S GERMAN JEWISH CONTRIBUTIONS

The German Jews who arrived in Milwaukee in the nineteenth century founded or helped found a battery of charitable organizations, educational services and fraternal groups to ensure their security in their new home and enhance city assets. These included the Hebrew Relief Society (today's Jewish Family Services), with its Coalition for Jewish Learning, that, today, supports Hillel Milwaukee and provides materials and workshops for city educational programming; a B'nai B'rith chapter that fights antisemitism; the Federated Jewish Charities (today's Milwaukee Jewish Federation) that supported the growth of Mount Sinai Hospital during the twentieth century; and the Jewish Home and Health Center.

Their focus on building city assets, as well as ensuring their own security, demonstrated the German Jews' commitment to Milwaukee. Rather than maintaining separatism, they promoted integration—both in the organizations they founded and through their synagogues—by holding regular Thanksgiving Day services and celebrating Washington's birthday.

Moses Annenberg represented this tendency of the Milwaukee German Jews to integrate into their surroundings. A transplant from Chicago, Moses sought avenues for his family to learn from other cultures and religions after he settled in Milwaukee.

THE ANNENBERGS: FAMILY OF COUNTERPARTS

In many ways, the Annenbergs were a family of opposites. Moses Annenberg, born in 1877, was the son of Jewish Orthodox immigrants from East Prussia. Growing up on the tough streets of south Chicago, Moses found a path into the Hearst Corporation as a circulation manager. Although he married a pious Jewish woman, Sadie Cecelia (née Freeman), Moses appeared to have liberal attitudes on religion.

Just after the turn of the century, Moses moved to Milwaukee and the Yankee Hill neighborhood to run the circulation department of *Wisconsin News*.[9] Having homes and offices both on Van Buren and Marshall, Moses soon began his own publishing and development business, M.L.A. Investment Co. of Milwaukee. He amassed a fortune quickly. His firm helped develop some of Milwaukee's landmark sites, including the historic Oriental Theater. As the publisher of *Daily Racing Form*, Moses took an avid interest in racetrack gambling and overtly cooperated with organized crime and the mafia. He eventually served time in prison for tax evasion.

Despite his own vices, Moses sought respectability for his children. In Milwaukee, he involved his family in German cultural life, even sending his sons to the German-English Academy (now the University School of Milwaukee), where they studied German language and customs. At home, the family surrendered kugel and latkes for schnitzel and Usinger's mortadella bologna.

Moses Annenberg sent his son Walter to a Baptist-run college-prep institution, Peddie School, in Hightstown, New Jersey, where Moses believed Walter would acquire discipline and respectability. In many ways, Walter matured to be very much the opposite of his father. He moved his father's publishing interests into wholesome mainstream media, such as *Seventeen* and *TV Guide*. He also took an immediate interest in public service and philanthropy and became one of the founding trustees of Eisenhower Fellowships. He was appointed by President Nixon as ambassador to the Court of St. James's in the United Kingdom. As a philanthropist, he gave persistently to Jewish causes, including a $15 million gift to Operation Exodus in 1990 to bring Russian Jews to Israel.

Walter Annenberg lived much of his adult life in New York and California. He was married twice—first to Bernice Veronica Dunkelman and then to Leonore "Lee" Cohn. He had two children with Bernice. Among the honors bestowed on Walter Annenberg for public service during his lifetime were the Presidential Medal of Freedom in 1986 and the Eisenhower Medal for Leadership and Service in 1988. He died in 2002.

TODAY'S MILWAUKEE JEWS

While most of the Jewish immigrants in the nineteenth century came from German-speaking areas of Europe, the later arrivals emigrated mostly from Eastern Europe. The settlement patterns also changed. The German Jews found homes downtown and on the east side, while the Eastern European Jews mainly settled first between Walnut Street and North Avenue west of the Milwaukee River and later in the Sherman Park neighborhoods. By the end of the twentieth and into the twenty-first century, most members of the earlier-arriving Jewish community had moved to the upper east side, Shorewood and the northern suburbs as far as Mequon in Ozaukee County. But pockets of Jewry remained in the city. A mostly secular wave of Russian Jews emigrated from the former Soviet Union in the late twentieth century and found a home around Oakland Avenue on the city's east side. A community of nearly two hundred families, led by the Twerskis—a nationally known family of Orthodox rabbis—settled in the Sherman Park area.

Jewish informants from Urban Anthropology's study of Milwaukee ethnic groups commented on the recent changes in the Jewish community.

There were two specific movements that happened in Judaism, which happened since the late 1960s. What you had in the 1960s in Milwaukee was a very strong periphery and a very weak core. You had a lot of Jews with an erosion of religiosity. One of the things that happened is that Jews gained greater freedom in America, which turned out to be the curse of intermarriage and assimilation, which occurred at that time. We were insulated from the factors of antisemitism. Today, you have a weak periphery and that core is very strong. The core is a dramatic growth of orthodoxy.

Most of the Orthodox keep their own version of Jewish culture by isolating themselves from others. The secular [Jews] struggle with this. If we are not particularly spiritual, where do we have culture?

With the shocking—yes, I say shocking—loss of Emanu El [Congregation Emanu-El B'ne Jeshurun], you've lost a lot of the social justice element of the Milwaukee German Jewish community. I remember Rabbi Barry Silberg. He had a show on Sunday morning, and it was always about some social issue. I'm sure that these Orthodox enclaves get deep meaning from their practices, but we also need that other element. What replaces it?

5

Forty-Eighters from German-speaking Nations

Milwaukee's Forty-Eighters were political refugees who fled Europe following the 1848 wave of revolutions that swept the continent. The uprisings were crushed by royal forces, leading to massive emigration, mainly from Germany and German-speaking areas in other countries. While there were only a few thousand who arrived in the United States, Milwaukee became one of their strongholds. Included among their numbers were "free-thinkers," writers and academics.

Forty-Eighter Footprints in Milwaukee

The Milwaukee Forty-Eighters organized effectively and quickly. Within five years, they'd helped form a number of progressive organizations, including the German English Academy (today's University School of Milwaukee). Many Forty-Eighters were involved in organizing the Milwaukee *Schulverein* (School Association) that promoted instruction in German as well as English. Besides language, the academy imported other German educational mainstays, such as singing, domestic science classes, drawing and physical education based on the German Turner movement.

The Milwaukee Turners was another Forty-Eighter product. The club, founded in 1853 as the "Socialist Turnverein," supported progressive policies and included among its members later Socialist congressman Victor Berger. With the slogan "a sound mind in a sound body," the local Turners

Turner Hall, which was completed in 1882 and designated a National Historic Landmark in 1996. Photograph taken circa 1890. *Milwaukee Turners collection*.

also focused on calisthenics and gymnastics. They built their clubhouse at 1034 North Fourth Street in Milwaukee's Westown neighborhood.[10] Still standing as a meeting and performance venue, the building is one of the largest associated with the Turner movement.

German informants in the Urban Anthropology Milwaukee ethnic study discussed the lasting impact of Turner Hall and the Turners in Milwaukee.

There's something almost mystical about being inside Turner Hall. You see the old photos on the wall—Zeidler winning the 1948 election, the balls they used to have for the Turners up in the ballroom, the charter of the Turners and everything they have stood for over the years. It is a most special feeling. It's Milwaukee, perhaps at its best.

I can say that you know Turner Hall is a good organization. The gymnastics. That sound mind and sound body that was taught and performed there eventually made its way into the Milwaukee public schools that decided that this was a good idea and had recess or gym. And so, it was not just the Turners anymore; it was the general school population that was exercising.

One of the great Milwaukee Forty-Eighters is highlighted below.

MATHILDE ANNEKE: A FOUNDER OF AMERICAN FEMINISM

Mathilde Anneke was arguably the most illustrious Forty-Eighter in the United States. She was a pioneer in the women's rights and suffrage movements. Born Mathilde Geisler into a wealthy German family in 1817, she received a liberal education and was married at the age of nineteen. She began writing at an early age. After experiencing a difficult divorce and custody battle over her children, she became interested in the cause of equal rights for women.

Mathilde later married Karl Friedrich Theodor "Fritz" Anneke, a Prussian officer, with whom she had several more children. His outspoken views cost him his position in the army. He was once imprisoned for eleven months on a charge of treason. From the beginning, the couple began taking up progressive activities. In Cologne, they published a newspaper for the working class. It was banned by authorities in 1847. Mathilde then founded the first German feminist journal, *Frauen-Zeitung*, which was also speedily banned.

When the 1948 revolution began, Fritz helped organize an artillery unit, and Mathilde worked as a mounted orderly. The revolts were quickly put down, and before the revolutionists surrendered, the couple fled to Switzerland, then France and then the United States. Settling in Milwaukee, Mathilde revived *Frauen-Zeitung* in 1850. The couple took the journal on the road to New York City and Newark, New Jersey, where Fritz began publishing a German American paper.

Back in Milwaukee, Mathilde and her children took up residence near Turner Hall in a home they shared with Sherman Miller Booth and his family. A kindred spirit to the Annekes, Sherman Booth was already known in Milwaukee as an abolitionist who'd received national attention for helping instigate a jailbreak for runaway slave Joshua Glover in violation of the Fugitive Slave Act. Booth would also be instrumental in forming the Liberty Party, the Free Soil Party and the Republican Party. And, like the Annekes, he was a publisher of progressive media.

The Annekes were also abolitionists. Fritz fought for the Union during the Civil War. He was commissioned a colonel in Company S, Wisconsin Thirty-Fourth Infantry Regiment, in late 1862 and was mustered out in late 1863 at Milwaukee's Camp Washburn.

The Annekes lived at various addresses in Milwaukee, including on Jefferson, North Ninth and Marshall Streets. In 1865, Mathilde founded the Academy for Young Women, which she directed until her death in 1884. Fritz had died earlier in 1870.

6.

THE POMERANIAN GERMANS
OF JONES ISLAND

During the 1870s and 1880s, a small wave of Pomeranian fisherfolk found their way to the Milwaukee area and settled on Jones Island, a strip of land surrounded by Lake Michigan and two rivers.

JONES ISLAND: AN ISLAND THAT IS ANYTHING BUT

Today, the Jones Island peninsula on Lake Michigan is a Milwaukee neighborhood and is currently home to Milwaukee's largest sewage treatment plant, warehouses, mountains of road salt, boxcars, railroad tracks, lift docks, petroleum tanks and a tiny park that commemorates the days when it was a fishing village.[11]

But why is a peninsula called Jones *Island*? The name derives from a Captain James Monroe Jones, who built a shipyard on the peninsula in the mid-nineteenth century. Over the years, the topography of the peninsula was altered by both human and natural forces. With a growth in commerce, lake vessels needed better access to Milwaukee's rivers, hence the city of Milwaukee completed a "straight cut" across the peninsula, eliminating nearly a mile of river channel for most appreciative lake captains. The straight cut severed the peninsula's connection to the mainland—hence came the designation "island." However, within a decade, storm waves filled the island's old river mouth with sand, and the island once again became a peninsula. But the name Jones Island persevered.

The Fishing Village: "The Damned Ducks Would Get Trapped in the Fishnets"

By the 1870s, a number of fisherfolk families from Europe had discovered the island was a fit place to earn their subsistence. These families included the Kaszubs from the Bay of Puck and the Hel Peninsula on the Baltic Coast of Poland, a handful of Scandinavians and Pomeranian Germans.

Most of the Germans who settled on Jones Island came from the fishing village of Altdamm on the Dammscher See, five miles from Stettin and about two hundred miles south of the Hel Peninsula. These Pomeranians had struggled with subsistence for generations and, during the late nineteenth century, faced the additional pressures of the Industrial Revolution, lack of sanitation, rampant unemployment and housing shortages. By 1870, some German fishing families immigrated to America and Jones Island. Most arrived in the 1880s.

Life was not much easier on the island. As squatters, they were not eligible for Milwaukee city services. And since they arrived with very little money, many of the fishermen initially relied on rowboats for their livelihoods, using set lines of pond (pound) nets. In 2001, Urban Anthropology Inc. conducted an oral history of Jones Island and interviewed the surviving members of the fishing village and their children. Many commented on the conditions on the island.

There was much isolation. People on the island were self-supporting, independent from the mainland. There was one cop from the city assigned to the island. That was it. You had gas lanterns for light at night and on the street. No plumbing. The houses were built everywhere, helter-skelter. There were no addresses, no grid of streets.

You got up early, worked late, went by a compass everywhere. It was very dangerous on the waters. Many drowned. On the way back, you would clean the nets out of fish so seagulls wouldn't follow you everywhere. When you came back, you had the reel for nets to let them dry. The kids' pastime was repairing nets.

There was no transport. No streetcar or bus. You paid 10 cents to row across the river. There was one milkman that came to the island. You did your washing in the river; we used Fels-Naptha soap to get the dirt out. You had your own chickens and goats and ducks. The damn ducks would get trapped in the fishnets all the time. There was a baker shop and a grocery on the island, but most everything came from home. We made our own sausages and butter, sewed our own shoes. Our water came from Lake Michigan or the Milwaukee River.

It was very tribal, with the Germans and Kaszubs. The Kaszubs spoke their own dialect of Polish, which wasn't understood by the mainland Poles. They went to St. Stan's church on Mitchell on the mainland. The Germans spoke low German and went to St. Peter's on Eighth and Scott.

But despite the difficult conditions, life in the fishing village was not without its charms.

Village Life: "Like the Wild West"

While the islanders' work and subsistence strategies were strenuous, so were their leisure-time activities. These included a baseball team, bonfires, dances, swimming, a German men's singing club, bands, religious holidays and a most robust tavern life. Informants from the oral history project described the nightlife.

There was a lot of drinking. Lots of taverns on the island. Dances every weekend. Fights broke out pretty often, and there were no police to stop them. That was common. It was a rough time, and they [islanders] worked hard and figured it was earned.

We all loved to drink and have fun. Every weekend, there were dances, and people would come from the mainland for the drinking and dancing and fish fries. The village had the reputation of being like the Wild West.

Just to ensure that the nightlife didn't overcome the day life, the islanders had their own forms of social controls. Their beliefs in supernatural forces extended beyond their Christian faith. Families consulted crystal balls and Ouija boards for guidance. Two women on the island were branded witches and were said to have powers to lay curses on anyone stepping outside the locally imposed boundaries.

The plethora of adult recreational activities on the island also drew mainlanders in large numbers. Many came to join in on the weekend revelries. Others were just curious about the villagers. A tour boat with mainland passengers would circle Jones Island, and the captain would point to the village, giving his version of what the fisherfolk's lives entailed. It was also common for art students, including poet Carl Sandburg, to visit the island on sketching trips. They'd produce renderings of the boats, the fish shanties, houses on stilts and the reels where the fisherfolk dried their nets.

THE LOSS OF THE FISHING VILLAGE

With the exuberance of life on the island, why did the fishing village disappear? The first threat to the village and its residents began as early as 1889, when the Illinois Steel Company, a huge iron mill just south of the settlement, sought better docking facilities for its fleet of lake ships. Illinois Steel tried to evict the fisherfolk from the northern half of Jones Island, using controversial claims based on tax deeds and the land title of a shipbuilding colleague of Captain Jones. The islanders, being mainly squatters, held no formal claims to their village. The battle with Illinois Steel raged on for nearly twenty years. Ultimately, the courts found irregularities in the company's claim to the land, and the village and most of its conflict-weary people stayed put—for a time.

But threats were to follow from another direction. The demands of the metropolitan area were beginning to encroach on the islanders' lives. Islanders then faced pressures from government. By the early years of the twentieth century, the bordering Milwaukee River had become a sewer. The City of Milwaukee decided to build a sewage treatment plant on the island and develop the island dock, and to do so, government officials had to condemn the fishing village in 1914. However, the city, unlike the steel company, was willing to pay the residents for the land. The islanders, perhaps exhausted by the long court battles or perhaps perceiving a futility in further confrontations, did not contest the city's eventual order to vacate the village. One by one, the residents began to move off the island. By 1920, only twenty-five families remained. The last islander to go was Felix Struck, who operated a tavern on the island until 1943. At the age of seventy-four, Struck and his family were formally evicted.

However, despite the loss of the village, the fishing vocation persisted for multiple generations among some of the island families, including the German Kriehns and Adrians.

THE KRIEHNS:
SETTLEMENT AIDED BY "BORROWED" PASSPORT

The Kriehn family operated fish markets on Jones Island and, later, on the Milwaukee mainland.

Born in 1828 in Germany, Karl Kriehn and his brother Franz came from a long line of Altdamm fishermen. Karl came to America in 1880. When he arrived on Jones Island, there were approximately twenty houses on the mile-long peninsula. He asked the islanders if he needed permission to build a house. His soon-to-be neighbors were squatters themselves and hence told him he did not. They said he could build wherever he wished. To accommodate his fishing vocation, Karl decided to construct his house near the river. When it was finished, he sent for his wife, Fredericka Kurt Kriehn, and the rest of his family.

Back in Altdamm, in 1882, Karl's brother Franz was still fishing. However, Franz's son Wilhelm had just turned twenty and was about to be conscripted into military duty. His father decided it was a good time to emigrate and join his brother. The duo decided they'd send later for Franz's wife, Caroline, and Wilhelm's fiancé, Louisa Habeck. However, the government officials

One of the Kriehn fish markets in the early twentieth century. *Ruth Kruehn collection.*

looking over the Kriehns' papers noted that Wilhelm had not completed his service, hence he was held back. With an alternative plan in mind for his son, Franz went ahead with his plan to immigrate to the United States. Back in Altdamm, Wilhelm "borrowed" a passport from a friend and soon joined his father in America. After arriving on Jones Island, the father and son ended up purchasing a house that was originally built by Valentine Struck, the first Kaszub to settle on the island. After a year in America, Franz and Wilhelm were fishing on a sailboat and were able to send for their women. Wilhelm then married Louisa Habeck in a Lutheran church on Mitchell Street. The couple remained on the island until well into the twentieth century.

Following the exodus of Kriehns from the island, Karl Kriehn's son Herman and Herman's wife, Minnie, opened a wholesale fish market on Twelfth Avenue (today's South Seventeenth Street). Karl's grandson Emil and Emil's wife, Caroline, opened a fish market on Third Street and Melvina.

THE ADRIANS: PARTNERSHIP WITH A KASZUB

The Adrians also operated at least one fish market.

Joseph John Adrian was born on Jones Island in 1886. His parents, Ludwig Adrian and Frances Grewald Adrian, had left Germany for the United States and Jones Island in 1880. As a boy, Joseph was quite industrious. He went to work for Tamms Fish Company when he was just thirteen, saving his money to purchase a tugboat called *Anna*. In 1918, while lifting nets from the tug, breakers came over the bow, broke all the windows and frames and thrust the boat miles into the lake. Joseph laid prone on the boat floor, having no idea where he was. Despite the dangers of his craft, by his early twenties, he was supporting his newly widowed mother and his siblings.

Eventually, Joseph started his own family. He married Elizabeth Warres. While still on the island, Joseph Adrian formed a partnership with another villager, Kaszub August Konkel. When eviction appeared imminent, the duo built a shanty at a bend in the Kinnickinnic River, on Milwaukee's mainland—an area that is, today, the corner of First and Becher Streets. The shanty became known as the Adrian and Konkel Fish Market. By 1930, Adrian and Konkel had purchased a diesel boat called *Irene*. Eventually, Joseph's son Frank began helping out with fishing and manning the market. Joseph died in 1948.

An anchor marking the presence of the fishing village on Milwaukee's Jones Island. *Urban Anthropology collection.*

THE FOOTPRINT LEFT IN THE
JONES ISLAND FISHING VILLAGE

What remains of this Pomeranian and Kaszubian settlement on the island? Certainly not people. In 1974, the City of Milwaukee constructed a tiny park on the island to commemorate the fishing village on the exact site of Felix Struck's tavern. An anchor from one of the original island ships, purportedly the SS *Lisa*, stands at the center of the 0.15-acre Kaszub Park. Each August, descendants of the original islanders hold a community-wide picnic, which is attended by seventy to eighty family members and others who are simply interested in learning more about them. The curiosity about the fishing village that once thrived in a large metropolitan area remains strong today among Milwaukeeans.

7.

GERMANS FROM RUSSIA
IN OLD NORTH MILWAUKEE

A culturally distinct German population began settling in North Milwaukee beginning around 1910, when the neighborhood (today's Old North Milwaukee) was still part of Granville Township.[12] The newcomers were Germans who had lived in Russia for generations—a population known as the German Russians or Germans from Russia.

THE RUSSIAN EXPERIENCE: A FREE LUNCH?

Beginning in the late eighteenth century, Catherine the Great and her son Czar Alexander had been trying to attract settlers to the Black Sea and Volga River areas of Russia. To anyone who could pay their own resettlement expenses, they would give land, religious freedom and, in some areas, exclusion from the draft and taxes. Often, entire villages moved together, maintaining the same village name in Russia as they had in Germany. Many Eastern European, Roma and Jewish groups also took advantage of the offer.

The Germans in both the Black Sea and Volga River regions maintained their settlements by religion. Most were either Catholic, Reformed or Lutheran, and a minority were Moravian, Mennonite and Jewish. In addition to the agricultural and economic opportunities, Russia allowed the German villages to remain isolated and hence retain their customs.

But over the generations, Russian leadership began to change their policies toward the Germans. Some of the early incentives from the czars were withdrawn—most particularly, the exemption from the Russian draft. A policy was also enforced to Russify the Germans—to compel all to speak Russian and follow Russian cultural traditions and religion. These changes were not received well by the German villagers.

THE ROAD TO MILWAUKEE: BUT NOT ALWAYS STRAIGHT

Beginning in the 1870s and well into the twentieth century, waves of Germans began emigrating from Russia. While some groups immigrated to places like Canada and South America, most came to the United States. Typically, the settlers from the Black Sea region ended up in the Great Plains states, where they engaged primarily in wheat farming, while the settlers from the Volga River migrated to the American West as well as the Great Plains.

The overwhelming majority of the German Russians that settled in the Old North Milwaukee neighborhood had come from the Volga River clusters and were Lutherans. They built Grace Lutheran Church (also known as Grace Lutheran Congregational Church) on North Thirty-Fourth Street, just south of Villard Avenue. But unlike many other German Russian settlements in the United States, the migration of this group from Russia to north Milwaukee was not always a straight line. Some of the first arrivals had come directly from Dreispitz Colony, but many others who ended up in the Milwaukee area had sojourned in other communities before arriving in the Old North Milwaukee neighborhood. The movement of the Zirgibel family is a good example of this migration pattern.

THE ZIRGIBELS: MANY STOPS ALONG THE WAY

Heinrich Zirgibel was born in 1869 in Russia—most likely in a German Volga River colony. His wife, Maria Jungmann Zirgibel, was born in 1875, also in Russia. They were both Lutherans. In 1898, the couple arrived in America. Following a brief stay in New York State, where their first child was born, they moved to Kansas, likely joining a German Russian community. There, two other children were added to the family.

By 1909, the young family had moved to Colorado. A job opportunity may have prompted the move. Along the lower Yellowstone River in Colorado and Montana, a large community of German Russians earned their livelihood in sugar beet fields. The demand for beets had been spurred by the Great Western Sugar Company, which was founded in Colorado in 1903. Great Western brought in both German Russian families and single Japanese men to help with the labors of sugar beet farming. While in Colorado, the Zirgibel family added two more children.

By 1915, the Zirgibels were in North Milwaukee. According to the 1920 U.S. Census, Heinrich was working as a farm laborer, and his family was living in a rented unit. Heinrich and Maria would remain in north Milwaukee until their deaths. The couple added five more children to the family between 1915 and 1926 and purchased a house on West Fairmount Avenue, just three blocks from Grace Lutheran Church. Heinrich died prior to 1930 and may not have lived to see the annexation of his German Russian settlement to the city of Milwaukee in 1929, where it became the Old North Milwaukee neighborhood. Maria, however, lived to be ninety and died in 1968, still residing in the same community.

Living with Diversity
"I Think the Term Is Ethnocentric"

By 1930, approximately 250 German Russian families lived in the Old North Milwaukee neighborhood. Gradually, a handful of families from the Black Sea colonies joined the Volga Germans. Both groups had been conditioned into a lifestyle of isolation from the rest of the local population back in Russia, a situation that helped them retain their ethnic identity. The fact that most arrived in communities already accustomed to isolation is unique from most other migrating groups, including those Germans who came directly from Germany. In fact, Germans from Russia in America have a reputation for adhering more rigidly to their traditions than their brethren who migrated directly from Germany. In the Milwaukee ethnic study conducted by Urban Anthropology Inc., descendants of this early German Russian community discussed not only the intensity of ethnic maintenance, but also the internal diversity.

I think the term is ethnocentric. The German Russians were very clannly. In fact, I'll tell you a story. An older cousin tape recorded some of our elders back in the 1960s. She asked about the people in our lineage. She was interviewing a great-uncle and then she asked about one woman—I won't say who. Then the uncle told her to turn off the tape recorder and told her that the relative was really a gypsy. For a long time, we thought maybe we had gypsies in our heritage, but we understood later that this was their way of signaling that the person was an outsider. She might have just come from a different German colony in Russia.

The German Russians from the Volga area would take pretty much any trade. They were hard workers. I think though that those that came from the Black Sea were more stubborn. I knew a lot of them growing up. They had to farm. They were going to be what they had always been. Had to own their land. And from what I've heard, even if they lost their land, they'd move in with relatives who had land. It was just so important.

My ancestors came from Ukraine in the Black Sea area and first settled in North Dakota before coming to the Milwaukee area. They were all farmers.... What I remember most from my grandmother was her use of women healers. The skills were passed down through women called brauchers. It was this thing they did blowing on the hand and called to the Father, Son, and Holy Ghost [demonstrates]. *They still do it in rural North Dakota. It's a really persistent tradition that not many people know about.*

But how did the German Russians interact with those outside of their own ethnic communities? As in Russia, they remained relatively isolated from their neighbors—both through choice and external prejudice. The isolation practices sometimes generated the suspicion of the surrounding communities. After the 1917 Bolshevik Revolution and growing communist paranoia in America, Milwaukeeans began calling the German Russian colony "Red Town," even though most of the Germans who'd arrived after the revolution loathed communism.

8.

DONAUSCHWABEN FROM
THE DANUBE REGION

*I*n 1722, Holy Roman Emperor Charles VI invited a group of German settlers to colonize mainly swampland areas that were bordered by the Danube, Tisza and Maros Rivers and the Carpathian Mountains in order to make the land agriculturally productive. At the urging of Charles VI's daughter and successor, Empress Maria Theresa, more Germans arrived between 1763 and 1770 and again in 1782. At the close of World War I, the areas where the Germans had settled were parceled out to Hungary, Romania and Yugoslavia.

Because most of the Germans farmed near the Danube, they gradually picked up the name of Danube Swabians, or Donauschwaben. Over approximately 150 years of settlement, the Donauschwaben continued to speak German and practice many of the traditions of their former homeland, but they also integrated into the fabric of their host countries—learning their languages and abiding by the local customs. All this changed during and after World War II. During Hitler's occupation of Yugoslavia, some Danube Swabians received preferential treatment. Some fought with the Germans—at times, under duress or conscription. Some fought with the royal Yugoslav army against the Germans.

When the war ended, the hatred for everything German turned on the Donauschwaben. Tito's forces in Yugoslavia imprisoned much of the Danube population, and 250,000 died in concentration camps. In Romania, some 75,000 Donauschwaben were forced to work in Soviet labor facilities, where about 11,000 died in the camps of the Ukraine and the neighboring

Urals. In 1951, others were rounded up from the remaining German villages and sent to the Baragan-Steppe in boxcars surrounded by soldiers with machine guns. Between 1951 and 1956, nearly 10,000 were deported, and approximately 1 in 15 lost their lives. In summary, there had been 1.6 million Donauschwaben living in Hungary, Yugoslavia and Romania in 1939, but by 1950, there were no more than 600,000.

Some of the few who survived immigrated to the United States. One was Anna Salm.

ANNA SALM NAEGELE: ESCAPING TITO, HITLER AND STALIN

Anna Salm was born in the town of Ernsthausen in Yugoslavia in 1931. Her family settled in Glogau in Banat State, near Belgrade. At the close of World War II, when Anna was just fourteen, President Tito's forces came to her town and conducted a house-to-house search for Germans. They cordoned off the German areas with barbed wire, and the police demanded to know the identity of their leaders. When no one responded, between four hundred and five hundred men were pulled out of their houses and shot. The remaining Donauschwaben were given twenty minutes to leave. They were then taken to a camp where they performed forced labor, and all they were given to eat daily was a slice of cornbread and a bowl of cabbage soup. Anna's father's job was to pull a wagon through the camp and remove the dead.

Telling her story to a *Milwaukee Journal* reporter in 1981, Anna described what happened next. Members of a camp family were planning an escape, and they agreed to take the Salm family along if they would carry the cargo. The escapees ran through the fields, often throwing themselves on the ground if they heard noises, and they eventually made their way to Hungary, where they found work. Unfortunately, the Russians were also rounding up Germans. The Salms were stopped by Soviet forces at the Austrian border. The Russians confiscated all their belongings but did not deport them to a Soviet work camp. The family eventually made it to a camp for displaced people, where Anna's mother was allowed to immigrate to the United States as a refugee. The rest of the family followed her in 1958.

Anna and her family settled in Milwaukee, where she was naturalized. She married a Milwaukee-born German, Heinz Neegele, and had two children. The family also lived for a time in Menomonee Falls and Brookfield in Waukesha County. Their daughter Rosemary, a graduate of Marquette University, became Miss Donauschwaben in 1981. Heinz died in 2005, and Anna died in 2015 at the age of eighty-four.

MILWAUKEE CHURCH AS SANCTUARY

Milwaukee's Midtown neighborhood, the home of the Second Ward Cemetery of the first wave of German immigrants, became a sanctuary for the city's last major wave of Germans to date.[13] St. Michael Parish was founded by Midtown neighborhood Germans in 1892. It had always been a place where new refugees found a spiritual home. When several hundred thousand Donauschwaben came to America at the end of World War II, many made their way to Milwaukee, and St. Michael's became the sanctuary site where the displaced Germans could restart their lives.

As the parish opened its doors to the Donauschwaben at the end of one war, it also became a sanctuary for Southeast Asians at the end of the Vietnam War. Hundreds of thousands of Hmong who faced genocide at the close of the war in Vietnam came to the United States late in the twentieth century. Milwaukee became a primary and secondary migration area, and St. Michael's welcomed them to the Midtown neighborhood, offering social services and masses in Hmong. More recently, the parish has opened its doors to recent immigrants from Myanmar (formerly Burma) who have arrived in Milwaukee after escaping conflict and discrimination in their native country. In addition, the parish offers services and mass in Spanish to accommodate Midtown's Latino population.

THE DONAUSCHWABEN TODAY:
"WHAT THEY SUFFERED KEEPS THEM TOGETHER"

Wanting to continue their traditions as they did along the Danube River, the Donauschwaben have worked diligently to support their local organization, United Donauschwaben of Milwaukee Inc., which was known previously as Tolnauer Komitat Vergnügungsverein and Donauschwaben Vergnügungsverein. Founded in 1945 by seventeen Danube Swabians, who had arrived in the United States earlier, membership increased dramatically in the 1950s and 1960s, when the refugee population flooded in. The organization formed major auxiliary groups over the years, and organized

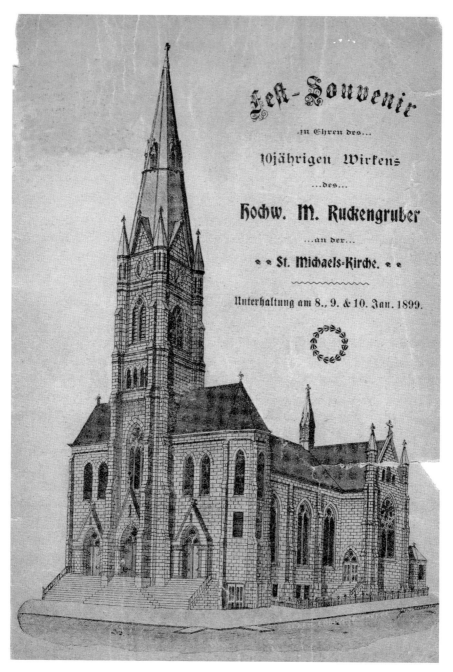

St. Michael's Catholic Church (today's St. Michael and St. Rose Catholic Parishes). Photograph from a souvenir booklet in 1899. *Milwaukee Archdiocese.*

performance groups and festivals. In 1966, the then–Donauschwaben Vergnügungsverein and three other Donauschwaben clubs joined forces and purchased the old Bert Philips Ballroom in Waukesha County and transformed it into a clubhouse. These allied clubs formed the United Donauschwaben of Milwaukee Inc. and named the facility the Schwabenhof.

While many Milwaukee German families and groups have lost their identity over the years, the local Donauschwaben remain united. During the twelve-year Milwaukee ethnic study by Urban Anthropology Inc., German informants offered explanations for their cultural coherence.

That's probably the only real cohesive German American population. Only because it has a high proportion of post-1945 immigrants and also because they suffered enormously with the expulsion process. Many of the Danube Germans were prisoners of the Soviets before they came to the United States. A friend of mine—who's approximately my same age—her mother starved to death in a concentration camp in 1947, and but for her grandmother who was there, she would have starved also in the expulsion process. It was very cruel and bitter. But that also unites people when you have common suffering, so there is a real strong sense among the Donauschwaben of cultural identity. That group hasn't assimilated to the same degree. They were expelled because they were perceived by the Yugoslavs, the Hungarians, the Slovacs, the Croatians [that] they were basically powerless. Germany was totally defeated. There was no other nation that could protect their national identity.

Most Americans have absolutely no idea about the whole history with that. There's a real reluctance from them to talk about it. They find it difficult to talk to the public about the whole victimization process that they went through because the opinion holds Germans responsible for the start of World War II.…There was no one there saying, "Oh my God, these poor women and children starved and [were] killed." But probably a good third of the Donauschwaben died in the expulsion process.

They don't like to talk about it because it's still the attitude that they were Germans during the war and such. So, I think what they suffered keeps them together—strongly together.

PART 2

German Place Names in Milwaukee Neighborhoods

9

NEIGHBORHOODS

*D*espite German hegemony in the development of Milwaukee, very few neighborhoods carry German names today. Most Milwaukee neighborhoods are designated by their physical characteristics, such as type of trees (e.g., Maple Tree), waterways (e.g., Menomonee River Hills), valleys (e.g., Mill Valley), glens (e.g., Hawthorne Glen), heights (e.g., Bluemound Heights), hills (e.g., Hillside), parks (e.g., Lake Park) and woods (e.g., Downer Woods). The following are three exceptions.

NEW COELN: A METHUSELAH OF MILWAUKEE NEIGHBORHOODS

Discussed in detail in part 1, the German Catholics from Cologne settled in a rural locale that would become a neighborhood on Milwaukee's south side. The long tenure of the settlers' descendants is probably the reason that the area retained its original name. This is also supported by the tenure of the New Coeln House, which was built in the late 1840s and still stands today.

At the time of this writing, Milwaukee's New Coeln neighborhood is one of thirteen that make up the city's Garden District.[14] While a relatively small number of Germans remain in the largely Latino, Polish and Muslim–dominated area, efforts have been made to honor the legacy of the region as an agricultural community. In 2008, Milwaukee's Common Council approved a resolution to name all the neighborhoods in the Thirteenth Aldermanic

The New Coeln House (circa 1912) on South Howell Avenue. Today, it is known as the Landmark 1850 Inn, Milwaukee's oldest saloon. *Landmark 1850 Inn.*

District the Garden District of the city of Milwaukee, capitalizing on a long tradition of gardening and farming among residents. At the time, Alderman Witkowski said, "Residents and businesses here have worked hard to solidify this identity. We have had perennial exchanges and gatherings, lectures by noted gardeners and even awarded area businesses landscaping awards to encourage and foster the character of our area."

The current incarnation of the New Coeln House, the Landmark 1850 Inn, remains vibrant. Now listed in the National Register of Historic Places, the bar specializes in eighteen beers on tap—from the local German variety to Belgian—with a food menu of sandwiches, appetizers, pizzas and a Friday fish fry (per the old German custom).

PIGSVILLE: HIDDEN CHARM
AND A SOUNDER OF SWINE

Pigsville is a small Milwaukee neighborhood south of Miller Valley that is practically hidden from view due to its location under the Wisconsin Avenue Viaduct.[15] While there is some debate about the origin of the neighborhood's name, most seem to agree that it came from one of the area's earliest settlers. Adam Freis, like many of his neighbors in the area, was born in Germany (in Hesse in 1850). He arrived in the United States with his wife, Louisa (née Rechlin); two young children; and his mother, Lisetta, in 1875. Freis worked for a few years in the milk trade in Milwaukee until he was able to purchase farmland in rural Wauwatosa on the banks of the Menomonee River (land that would later be annexed to Milwaukee). Freis made an unusual decision for the area—he decided to farm pigs.

Adam Freis steadfastly enlarged the farm. Even after his wife died, his children remained involved in the pig farm until his sounder of swine reached two hundred. People in the bordering neighborhoods made remarks about

Pigsville neighborhood, circa 1988. *Alan Maganye-Roshak collection.*

the large number of pigs grazing on the right bank of the Menomonee River. While many believe that this is where the name Pigsville originated, various versions of the name (Piggsville, Pigsville, Pigville and the Valley) were widely used until decades later. Pigsville is the official name of the neighborhood today.

MACK ACRES: A CARPENTER'S SUBDIVISION

Milwaukee's Mack Acres neighborhood owes its current existence to a building contractor named Rudolph "Rudy" Mack.[16] Born in 1896, Rudy was raised in and around the Granville area, which, today, encompasses much of Milwaukee's northwest side. His family lived at various times on Hopkins Street, Fond du Lac Avenue and in the town of North Milwaukee (today's Old North Milwaukee neighborhood). He was the son of German immigrants Rudolph Mack and Louisa Reichow.

Rudolph Sr. was an industrious man. While living on Hopkins Street, he opened a grocery store. A decade later, he started his own building construction business. As Rudy Jr. entered his teen years, he worked as a carpenter for the firm. But in 1918, while the United States was in World War I, Rudy enlisted, serving in the U.S. Army for the duration of the conflict.

On his return, Rudy Jr. returned to his father's business. He eventually married a woman with the same first name as his mother—Louisa—née Schroeder. During the Great Depression, when the building trade came to a halt, Rudy settled for a supervisory job for a government program, possibly the Works Progress Administration (WPA). At the end of the Great Depression and World War II, the building trade resurged. Rudy resuscitated his father's contracting business and developed the subdivision that would later be known as Mack Acres. Rudy died in 1971.

One of the streets in Mack Acres was originally christened Mack Avenue. However, in 1956, the homeowners petitioned for a name change, arguing that it was too closely identified with Mack Trucks. Thus, today, the street is called Beechwood Avenue.

10.

STREET NAMES

As with neighborhoods, surprisingly few Milwaukee streets were christened after Germans. Like in other cities, many Milwaukee streets were named after locations, such as U.S. states and cities (e.g., Wisconsin Avenue, St. Paul Avenue). Other streets were named after historic figures, like American presidents (e.g., Washington Boulevard, Lincoln Avenue). And still others were christened by land developers who built roads and quickly bestowed on them their own surnames or those of their family members. However, in the latter case, multisyllabic German names were sometimes Anglicized in subsequent generations. The following is one example that failed.

MEINECKE AVENUE AND THE NAME GAME

Born in 1830 in Oldenburg, Germany, Adolph Meinecke arrived in the United States in 1847. He had moved to Milwaukee by 1855. Adolph and his wife, Marie Louise (née Kraft), opened a "fancy goods" store in the downtown area. They must have done reasonably well because, according to the U.S. Census, the couple had already bought a house on Huron by 1860, where their children, two of their store clerks and a servant also lived.

The Meineckes eventually purchased a thirty-seven-acre lot of willow fields near Fifteenth Street and North Avenue in today's North Division neighborhood, where they founded Milwaukee Willow Works, a factory that produced furniture, wicker baskets and toys.[17] In 1887, Adolph named one street that went through their lot Meinecke Avenue. He donated some of the land to the City of Milwaukee for a firehouse but stipulated that if the name of the street was ever changed, the land's ownership would revert back to his family.

But the name did change. City officials, probably seeking street names that were easy to pronounce and spell, changed Meinecke Avenue to Lee Street within a few decades. However, in 1927, the Meinecke couple's grandson Ferdinand Meinecke, apparently having access to the original agreement, pointed out the provision in his grandfather's donation. Given that the land was then worth over $100,000, city officials recognized their error in judgment and very quickly changed the street name back to Meinecke Avenue.

AUER AVENUE: "THE BABY FLAT LANDLORD"

There's something about a neighborhood. Take Riverwest. You always know who's going to move there, live there—who's going to die there. When I tell people that I come from Riverwest, people know what they're getting. It's someone really concerned about social issues, the arts, diversity, activism, social justice.

The preceding quote belongs to a neighborhood informant in Urban Anthropology's oral history of Milwaukee's Riverwest neighborhood.[18] As the quote implies, Milwaukee's Riverwest residents have long histories of social activism—from the early German and Polish occupation to the counter-cultural era of the 1960s and 1970s. Today's diverse neighborhood has a mix of liberal European Americans, Puerto Ricans and African Americans. This ethos was also true of the namesake of Riverwest's Auer Avenue.

Louis Auer Jr. was born in 1857 in Milwaukee. His parents, Louis Auer Sr. and Christine Hartung, were German immigrants from Baden. According to the 1860 U.S. Census, the couple operated a small hotel and boardinghouse in the downtown area when Louis Jr. was a toddler. Louis Sr. eventually gave up the hotel for the insurance business and later went into public life, becoming an alderman, county supervisor and school commissioner.

Louis Jr. went into real estate, where he prospered. He married Jane Stewart Holohane later in life and had at least three children. In the 1900 Census, the Auer family is listed as living on State Street, with two small children, a nurse, servant and a coachman in the household. Perhaps it was Louis Jr.'s experience with becoming a new parent in his forties that led to his concern for the welfare of families. As a developer, he believed it was unfair that so many landlords refused to rent to couples with children. Hence, he built apartments designed for children with soundproof floors, courtyards and playgrounds, giving families free rent on any month a baby was born. One of the streets where he built these units originated in the Riverwest area, and he named it Auer Avenue in 1888.

Called "the baby flat landlord," Louis Jr.'s activism did not stop with families. He became a general in the Wisconsin National Guard, served as a member of Milwaukee's Park Commission and was a vocal advocate for Milwaukee-made products. He died in 1910.

ADLER STREET AND A NAMESAKE WHO WALKED FROM CHICAGO TO MILWAUKEE

Adler Street, platted in 1888 by Frederick Theodor Christian Adler, is in Milwaukee's Johnson's Woods neighborhood.[19] Born in 1839 in Plath, Mecklenburg, Germany, Frederick Adler arrived in the United States with his parents in 1852. The family sojourned briefly in New York and Chicago, when, at the age of fifteen, young Frederick walked from Chicago to Milwaukee. He stayed in a boardinghouse in the Third Ward and worked as a railroad porter. In 1861, Frederick married Emilie Filter, the daughter of Prussian immigrants.

Naturalized in 1871, Frederick Adler began working in a bank, first as a clerk and later as a bookkeeper. He invested in real estate, including acreage in Johnson's Woods, where he platted Adler Street. He served as a City of Milwaukee alderman during the 1870s. By 1880, the couple, who had never had children, purchased a home on Fifth and Walnut and later moved farther west to Twenty-Fifth Street. Emilie died in 1912, and Frederick died in 1929.

BETTINGER COURT AND A NAMESAKE WHO WALKED FROM BUFFALO TO MILWAUKEE

Like Adler Street, Bettinger Court in Milwaukee's Clarke Square neighborhood owes its name to a man who walked a great distance to get to Milwaukee.[20] Nicolaus Bettinger, born 1820 in Germany, arrived in Buffalo, New York, in 1840. One year later, he and five of his cousins walked to Milwaukee. After marrying Angela Brachman in 1850, the

Remains of a red brick wall of Bernhard Leidersdorf's historic mansion. *Urban Anthropology collection.*

couple purchased a home on Pierce Street, where they had six children. Over the years, Nicholas worked as a trapper, hunter and brickmaker and also set up a saloon near his residence. He died in 1896, leaving the tavern to his son John G.

John G. married Mary Schramm in 1878, and the couple had seven children. The block where the saloon was located, between National Avenue and Pierce Street, included nine cottages and a hotel. By the early years of the twentieth century, the tiny street had become known as Bettinger's Court—a name that was later officially recognized. In his retirement years, John G. moved to Greenfield, where the family purchased a farm. He died in 1915.

Less than two blocks from Bettinger's Court, another German immigrant left a footprint that is still visible in Clarke Square today. By the late 1800s, the section of National Avenue that was within the Clarke Square boundaries had become a south side gold coast, lined with mansions of the wealthy. The most significant estate belonged to a German-born Jew (albeit, he was baptized Lutheran) named Bernhard Leidersdorf, whose land comprised six acres on National, between Seventeenth and Eighteenth Streets. The fully staffed estate included its own lake, a grove of trees imported from Europe and a red brick wall that remains today. Leidersdorf died in 1912, and gradually, the street evolved into a business corridor accompanied by rows of apartments.

CAROL STREET:
NAMED AFTER A MEMORABLE CHRISTMAS

In 1927, developer Arthur Wenz's real estate company built a subdivision at the southern tip of Milwaukee's Bay View neighborhood.[21] The descendant of immigrants from Wurttemberg, Germany, Wenz was born in Wisconsin in 1880. He married Madeline Zinn and had daughters Carol Lenore and Lolita Gertrude. Arthur began work as a fire insurance agent. The couple apparently lived frugally while Arthur built up his real estate business, as the U.S. Census had the family living with Madeline's parents on Shepard Avenue in 1920.

Several years later, Arthur Wenz's company was developing the Bay View subdivision. Arthur named one street Carol—"after a Christmas Carol," quipped one Bay View informant during a 2013 oral history of the neighborhood. The remark bore some truth, as Wenz's daughter Carol Lenore Wenz had been born on Christmas Day in 1907.

WAHL AVENUE:
"THE FATHER OF MILWAUKEE'S PARK SYSTEM"

Wahl Avenue runs along Lake Park in Milwaukee's Northpoint neighborhood.[22] It was aptly named after the man who became known as the "Father of Milwaukee's Park System"—Christian Wahl.

Born in Bavaria in 1829, Christian Wahl came to America with his parents in 1846. The family settled in the Town of Lake, a village that would later be annexed to Milwaukee. Christian married Antoinette Guenther, and the couple had three children. They moved to Chicago, where Wahl developed a glue factory. As the factory became a success, Wahl became interested in public life and assumed several leadership positions in Chicago. However, sometime after 1880, Wahl retired from the glue factory and decided to return to his childhood home.

After returning to Milwaukee, the Wahls purchased a home on Prospect Avenue. He resumed his interest in public life and joined the Milwaukee Park Commission, taking on the role of president between 1889 and 1899. He led most of the planning processes of the county's park system and was instrumental in the development of Lake Park on the shores of Lake Michigan. The park's architect was Frederick Law Olmsted, who was chiefly known for designing New York City's Central Park. Wahl helped plan the rustic footbridge across the southern ravine in 1895.

The bust of
Christian Wahl
at Wahl Park.
*Urban Anthropology
collection.*

Wahl died in 1901. Following his death, city officials named the street that
ran along Lake Park Wahl Avenue. Milwaukeeans also erected a monument
of Christian Wahl that was designed by Gaetano Trentanove; it was unveiled
in 1903, originally in front of the Lake Park pavilion. This monument was
later moved to another park.

In 1956, many miles to the northwest of Lake Park, a twelve-acre green
space was named after Christian Wahl and became Wahl Park. By 1960, the
Lake Park bust was moved to Wahl Park. The area surrounding the park was
then named Wahl Park.[23]

SCHLINGER AVENUE: NOT YOUR TYPICAL NAMESAKES

Schlinger Avenue originates in Milwaukee's Fair Park neighborhood.[24]
However, the street's namesakes had about as little to do with the fairgrounds
as they had to do with wildlife conservation. The Schlinger brothers (also

spelled Schlenger) were celebrated locally as calculating wolf hunters. Michael, born in 1842, and George, born in 1856, were the children of Georg Schlenger and Maria Degan Schlenger, who had brought their large family to the Milwaukee area from Hessen, Germany, in the early 1850s. The family settled for a time on a farm near what is now Ninety-Second Street and Schlinger Avenue in the old town of Wauwatosa.

While working as farmhands and coopers, the two brothers took up the hobby of wolf hunting. But their hunting was not confined to their own neighborhood. At the request of local sheep farmers miles from the Milwaukee area, they took their vocation to suburbs such as Elm Grove, where the media followed their arduous hunts for days. Even their dog was celebrated. It was purported to be the offspring of an infamous slave-hunting bloodhound, and the brothers entertained offers of hundreds of dollars for the canine's sale.

However, by the 1880s, the declining wolf population in the Milwaukee area forced the brothers into other locales. The entire Schlinger family moved to the town of Cherokee in Cherokee County, Iowa, by 1885, where the brothers remained until their deaths.

In 1926, the old town of Wauwatosa moved to name the street just north of Wisconsin State Fair Park after the Schlinger brothers—for reasons unknown. The fairgrounds were originally built in 1891, when the Wisconsin

The entrance to State Fair Park (circa 1910), near Schlinger Avenue. *West Allis Historical Society.*

State Agricultural Society purchased a large dairy farm owned by a Stevens family. However, two years later, the entire estate burned to the ground, and new buildings had to be erected. When, in 1894, the Milwaukee Street Car Company extended its lines to the newly built fairgrounds, more people accessed the fair, and the area to the north of State Fair Park began to fill up with settlers.

PART 3

Remains of German Commerce in Milwaukee Neighborhoods

11.

Shopping Hubs

According to the December 1, 1932 edition of the *Milwaukee Journal* (page 33):

Few, if any, cities in America have as many trading centers as Milwaukee. Although Upper Third Street is as important of [sic] *the neighborhood business centers and serves one of the largest districts, every section of the city has its own local trade area.*

With as many neighborhood commercial districts as Milwaukee once had, there were very few that weren't developed chiefly by Germans. Obvious exceptions would be Lincoln Avenue and Historic Mitchell Street on Milwaukee's south side in the Polish area of the city. However, some neighborhood shopping hubs had more lasting impacts than others.

NORTH THIRD STREET: THE "GERMAN DOWNTOWN"

North Third Street was once known as the "German downtown" of Milwaukee. Today, the street is divided into two sections with different names: Dr. Martin Luther King Jr. Drive and Green Bay Avenue. Most of the middle section of the street was once called "Upper Third Street" and marks the boundaries between the Harambee, Riverwest and Brewer's Hill neighborhoods.[25]

The anchor of Upper Third was Schuster's Department Store. Edward Schuster, a German Jew, was born in 1832 in Germany. After immigrating to the United States and Milwaukee, he opened a dry goods store (a nineteenth-century term for textiles and ready-to-wear clothes) on North Third Street and soon followed with two more branches. He died in 1904, but his son-in-law, Albert Friedmann, maintained the tradition of conducting business in Milwaukee's residential neighborhoods rather than downtown. He opened three multistory stores, one on North Third and Garfield, one on Eleventh and Historic Mitchell and one on Twelfth and Vliet. Schuster's soon became Milwaukee's premier department store, even though the family never opened a store on Wisconsin Avenue.

A block away from Schuster's, on the corner of North Third and North Avenue, was Rosenberg's Fine Apparel. Rosenberg's was founded by Abraham Peter "A.P." Rosenberg, who ran it until his retirement in 1927. Nearby was Bitker-Gerner's, another apparel shop operated by Pierce Henry Bitker and his wife, Thelma. While these entrepreneurs were Jewish with ancestry in Russia, most merchants on Upper Third had German roots. Among them was a group of immigrants with saloons in the middle of the twentieth century, including German immigrant Paul F. Winkelman with the tavern at 1731 North Third, German immigrant Minnie Kreiter with the tavern at 1745 North Third and German immigrant Wentzel Gilch with the tavern at 1835 North Third.

There were also a good number of female-owned shops on Upper Third. In the 1930s, these shops included Mitzi's Hats, Frieda Herrann Restaurant, Dressmaker Mrs. Christine Makoski, Rosella Beauty Shop, Lillian Hat Shop, Ida J. Seyferth Draperies, Florine's Lady's Ready-to-Wear, Dressmaker Irene Love, Mrs. Florence Winthrop Tavern & Billiards and more.

Altogether, there were over three hundred stores in the district by the 1930s, and most of the shops' façades exhibited careful attention to architectural detail. In 1918, the Upper Third Street Commercial Association was formed and drew one hundred members by 1931. With the help of the association, the district survived the Great Depression. Organizing promotions such as Milwaukee Day on December 2, the store owners and the association collaborated to reduce prices to the lowest they had ever been. Also, in order to help the unemployed, store owners hired many residents as "sandwich men," who paraded large advertising placards along the streets.

Throughout the Great Depression, World War II and postwar years, store owners continued to cooperate and attract consumers. Changes began with the proliferation of the automobiles during the 1950s. Parking on Upper

Rosenberg's Department Store on North Avenue and Third Street (*see the building with a tower*) in 1949. *Milwaukee Public Library, Remember When Collection, RW 1908.*

Third became a problem when shoppers began to rely less on streetcars and busses and more on their family cars to take them to stores. Strip malls also began to draw consumers. In 1956, the Capitol Court Shopping Center opened on Sixtieth Street and Capitol Drive. Within three years, Upper Third Street lost nearly 40 percent of its business. Rosenberg's and Bitker-Gerner's closed their doors, along with scores of other stores. Schuster's survived because of its presence in Capitol Court, but sales at their Third Street store dropped dramatically.

By the 1960s, Upper Third was a shopping hub of the past. The neighborhood had also changed. At the time, African Americans dominated the north side. On November 13, 1984, a group called the Young Milwaukeeans presented a petition to the aldermen on Milwaukee's Common Council, with seventeen thousand signatures backing a name change of Third Street to Dr. Martin Luther King Jr. Drive. After much deliberation, the full council voted thirteen to three to rename the street, but with the following compromise: the stretch from West Wisconsin Avenue, north to West McKinley Avenue, would become North Old World Third Street, while Third Street from McKinley to West Capitol Drive would be renamed to honor King. The section of street north of Capitol Drive would become Green Bay Avenue. Mayor Henry Maier signed the resolution.

Since the change in name, new developments have been added to Martin Luther King Jr. Drive. A Business Improvement District (BID) was opened on the historic street in 1992. In the following fifteen years, more than $400 million of development was added, including over sixty businesses operated by culturally diverse entrepreneurs. The street also assumed a distinct African American quality when the section of the drive between North Avenue and Burleigh Street was reserved every June 19 for the celebration of Juneteenth Day.

Are there remaining footprints of the once-strong German presence on the street? According to informants in Urban Anthropology's twelve-year study of Milwaukee's ethnic groups, the answer is yes. The careful attention to architectural detail that so aptly distinguished the street is still very present.

On Martin Luther King Jr. Drive, you'll see a stretch of street that clearly was the local shopping district back then, where now, everyone goes to the malls or Target or something. But you will see a block area where you can tell that this was a corner tavern, and you will see the copulas and the open domes around the building or the corner door and the moldings and a lot of the attention to detail. Even a small building was designed to be attractive. So, someone who was building even a corner grocery shop didn't just put up cheap siding. They had stone, and they had someone make a point to make certain patterns and stuff like that.

When you look at today's MLK [Martin Luther King Jr. Drive]—then Third Street—you can't help but notice how well those buildings have stood the test of time. They are absolutely works of art. This tells you something about our early tradition of German architecture. And no one is letting these buildings go to hell. You walk down Martin Luther King Jr. Drive, and you see how well these business owners are preserving the buildings.

Vliet Street: Christmas Floats on Rails

The four-and-one-half-mile commercial corridor of Vliet Street extends from about North Seventh on the east side to the Wauwatosa boundary of North Sixtieth Street to the west, and it once encompassed some of the densest shopping hubs in Milwaukee. A major draw to the street's west end was Washington Park and the Washington Park Zoo. Designated locally as the boundary between Milwaukee's west side and north side, today, Vliet Street runs through the neighborhoods of Park View, King Park, Midtown, Cold Spring Park, Martin Drive and Washington Park.[26]

Just as one Schuster's store had become the anchor for Upper Third Street, another served as an anchor for the east end of Vliet Street. Opening in November 1937, the new department store at Twelfth and Vliet promised to serve a population of over 300,000. The building featured two rotunda staircases that led from the first level to a housewares floor and a dinette that seated 146. By 1938, the new Schuster's had become a cornerstone in the businesses' Advancement Association that included 329 stores between Seventh and Twelfth Streets on Vliet and a corridor on North Twelfth Street.

But Schuster's became more than a commercial anchor. The Schuster's Christmas Parade soon became a defining feature of the local holiday season and of Vliet Street generally. Beginning in 1927, the parade ran on the rails of the city streetcars. Floats depicting fairytale and Disney characters moved through the neighborhoods on electric flatcars. Live reindeer rode on the cars. The parade route went from the west end of Vliet Street at Washington Park to Twelfth Street, where it turned south through parts of the downtown area and south again on Second Street to Mitchell. The climax of the parade was, of course, Santa, but Milwaukeeans made a celebrity out of one of his helpers, Billie the Brownie. For weeks before the parade ensued, locals would follow the reports of Billie on WTMJ Radio, charting the movements of Santa Claus and his entourage. The last parade was held in 1961.

Vliet Street served all its neighborhoods with grocers, gas stations, clothing stores, restaurants, dry cleaners, hardware stores, real estate agencies, taverns, bakeries, butchers and banks. One of the key enterprises on the west end of Vliet Street, across from Washington Park, was H. Militzer Quick Service, an Independent Grocers Alliance (IGA) grocery store run by German immigrant Herman Militzer. Born in 1887 in Tanna, Germany, Herman immigrated to the United States and Milwaukee in 1906. He worked as a waiter for over a decade and lived in boardinghouses on the near north side. Sometime before 1919, he married Mary Rostetter, and the couple rented a storefront and living quarters at 4301–4303 West Vliet Street. There, they opened the grocery store and raised a small family.

When the IGA was founded in 1926, the Militzers joined. Herman served at least one term as president and no doubt played some role in bringing

IGA convention banners (1941) at H. Militzer Quick Service. *Pat Mueller collection.*

the IGA convention to Milwaukee in March 1941. Two thousand delegates attended the event at the Milwaukee Auditorium, and local grocers such as the Militizers hung banners over their stores throughout the city.

According to Militizer descendants, the family had a ritual for disposing of vegetables that had passed their prime. It was the task of Militizer children (and, later, the grandchildren) to offer wilting produce to the animals at the zoo at Washington Park. Feeding heads of cabbage to the hippos was a particularly common practice and a popular one for children to watch.

As with Upper Third Street, the proliferation of the automobile played a key role in the eventual decline of Vliet Street as a major Milwaukee shopping hub. Parking became a problem along the street, and consumers began to choose strip malls and shopping centers as more convenient places to purchase their goods. But the rise of the automobile also meant more highways. The construction of I-43 stripped away all stores between Tenth and Twelfth on Vliet and most of the Twelfth Street corridor. On the west end, the stadium freeway unearthed the section of Washington Park where the zoo had been located, and the buildings and animals were moved to the city's edge on Bluemound Road.

Informants in the neighborhood oral histories of Urban Anthropology Inc. lamented these changes and their impacts on both ends of Vliet Street.

> *The freeway was coming through. Schuster's* [on Twelfth and Vliet] *closed, I believe, in 1961. If we hadn't figured out what was happening to our street by then, we sure would soon. Schuster's—that great building—ended up becoming the Milwaukee Welfare Department, where the poorest of poor came to sign up for aid and collect their checks. A few years after that came the homeless shelters on that block.*

> *You're going to ask me about the freeway. There were houses behind us,* [and] *behind there was the zoo. You could walk down Forty-Sixth and cross Vliet and you were on the zoo grounds. The building closed, but the zoo was always open because of the park. We could hear the lions roar if the wind was coming from the right direction. I remember Samson and Sambo* [gorillas] *when they were babies, and the lady caring for them was in the cage dressed as a nurse.*

Following the construction of the freeway, much of the east end of Vliet Street was set aside for public housing. Today, the Schuster's building is the Marcia P. Coggs Human Service Center.

On the street's west end, organizations have remained at work to keep the business corridor viable, as they no longer have the popular zoo as a draw. These organizations include the Near West Side Business Improvement District and the Wisconsin Women's Business Initiative Corporation. According to Vliet Street Work Group cochair Pat Mueller, the Business Improvement District has expanded opportunities for small business entrepreneurs. "A long-stagnant part of West Vliet Street has seen great small-scale development," said Mueller, "especially in the 3800 block of West Vliet." The façades on the entire block were redone. Four new businesses were opened, and a new owner-operator of Sanders Bowl is "breathing

The former Schuster's building remains a footprint of the once-dominant business corridor on the east end of Vliet Street. Today, it is the Marcia P. Coggs Human Service Center. *Urban Anthropology collection.*

life into the age-old pastime of bowling." Mueller continued, "Neighbors are excited and are strongly supporting these businesses. We are hoping to expand that momentum further on the street."

WEST BURLEIGH STREET: GROWING UP AT THE MOVIES

West Burleigh Street has been the major commercial corridor in the Sherman Park area on Milwaukee's northwest side. Today, Sherman Park comprises the neighborhoods of St. Joseph, Grasslyn Manor, Roosevelt Grove, Sunset Heights, Uptown and Sherman Park.[27]

Residents began to settle Sherman Park in the first two decades of the twentieth century. Many were attracted to the suburban look of the area on the edge of the city. Developers had created wide, tree-lined streets and boulevards, but the beautiful homes were the neighborhood's signature. The large bungalows, duplexes and Period Revival homes were finely crafted from brick, wood and stone.

The first arrivals to the area were primarily Germans and Czechs who were migrating from various Milwaukee neighborhoods. Later migrants were diverse populations, representing over twenty nations from nearly every continent. The largest of the later-arriving groups were Jews and African Americans.

West Burleigh quickly developed as the major shopping hub of the area—particularly, the blocks between North Thirty-Fifth and North Sixtieth Streets. While the merchants in the corridor were relatively diverse, Germans historically dominated. For example, in 1940, the first block of the Burleigh hub between Thirty-Fifth and Thirty-Sixth Streets included the following merchants: Andrew Schwister, a shoe merchant and the grandson of Prussian immigrants; Joseph Braunweiter, a saloon keeper and German-speaking immigrant from Czechoslovakia; and William Klunder, a deli merchant and the son of a German immigrant. Moving west ten blocks to Forty-Fifth Street, the area between Forty-Fifth and Forty-Sixth included the following merchants: Emile C. Horn Drugs, a druggist and the grandson of German immigrants; Edward Zoeller, a grocer and the son of a German-speaking Austrian; John Gleich, a baker and the son of German immigrants; Hugo Kneer, a saloon keeper and the son of German immigrants; Walter Liermann, a shoe repairman and German immigrant; and Martin Kramarich, a saloon keeper and German-speaking immigrant from Austria.

During Urban Anthropology's oral history of the Sherman Park–area neighborhoods, long-time residents stressed the importance of being able to walk to shops on West Burleigh. And it wasn't just to meet their material needs, it was also to socialize and be entertained. Along the street were bowling alleys, restaurants, taverns, faith communities and delis. By 1935, the area had three theaters. The first to open in 1921 was the Parkway, located blocks south of the Sherman Park area on Thirty-Fifth and Lisbon. The second was the Uptown, which was opened in 1926 on Forty-Ninth and North Avenue, within the Sherman Park area. The last, the Sherman Theater, was most unusual because it was opened in the middle of the Great Depression in 1935, at 4632 West Burleigh Street, also within the Sherman Park area. The Graylock Investment Company decided to build a commercial strip between Forty-Sixth and Forty-Seventh Street on Burleigh, with the theater as the centerpiece. It became known for showing films in Yiddish through the mid-1950s. Informants in the Sherman

Park oral history project discussed the importance of the theaters to the community—particularly, its younger members.

> *Each movie theater was different. Generally, Uptown was for the high school kids….Parkway was for junior high school kids, and the Sherman Theater on Burleigh was also for junior high school kids, but mostly, the Jewish kids hung out there. It was the center of the Jewish neighborhood.*

> *Sherman Theater, in the days before television, you didn't have to go downtown to see theater. You just walk a few blocks and go to the Sherman. It was walkable.*

> *And I don't know when the adults went to the theaters 'cause they sure as hell weren't there when we were there. Not if they wanted to keep their sanity. But on those days—on a Friday night or a Saturday day—that was when those theaters were specifically [open] for that age group. That was how the owners designed it. They got the movies that way, and they made money that way. When we were little grade-school kids back then, we had the 25-cent cartoon Saturdays, with Roy Rogers and Hopalong Cassidy and the Dark Shadow—the guy with the black hat and [the guy with] the black cape.*

As with the other shopping hubs, West Burleigh Street declined as the automobile grew in popularity. Shoppers chose the strip malls and shopping centers with greater access to parking. But the residents of Sherman Park did not acquiesce when the county announced that the Park West Freeway would be constructed through their neighborhood. They banded together, fought the effort for years and ultimately prevented the progress of the highway.

Today, there are a number of efforts afoot to keep the West Burleigh commercial corridor viable. Among them is the Burleigh Street Community Development Corporation. Taking renewed interest in the Sherman Theater, the City of Milwaukee called for its redevelopment in 2009 in its west side comprehensive plan. Partnering in the effort, the Burleigh Street Community Development Corporation brought the theater online in 2012 with the hopes of generating interest in creating a center for the visual, musical and performing arts, with space for studios, galleries and offices.

12.

OTHER RETAIL

S chuster's, which was discussed in part 3, had been Milwaukee's beloved department store. It would only be rivaled by one other—also founded by a German Jew.

GIMBELS DEPARTMENT STORE: MODELS WITH MIDRIFF BULGE

When Gimbels first took over Schuster's, we all thought it was going to be terrible. But Gimbels proved to be just as good a store. I used to sew all the clothes for my kids and would go to their fabric department on the fourth floor. And the clerks got so used to me that they'd direct me right to the new fabrics that they thought I'd like. Then, when my son was born and it was hard to get out to shop, I would just call these clerks. I'd set up the order over the phone because, by now, they knew my tastes. Then it would be delivered the next day. Service was simply as good as it could be.

We loved the downtown Gimbels. The quality of anything you'd buy was the best. Way up on the top floor, they had a very nice restaurant. I think they called it the Forum or something like that. They'd have fashion shows there. [Laughs] My friends and I would go. There were fashion shows with runway models I think over the noon hour. The models of that time had midriff bulge and little tummies. This was back around

1970. You wouldn't see that today. But those of us who went to the shows loved it—they looked a little like us.

The preceding quotations are from Urban Anthropology's neighborhood oral history projects. In 1962, Gimbels acquired its Milwaukee competitor, Schuster's, which still had stores open on Upper Third Street in today's Halyard Park neighborhood, Historic Mitchell Street in the Historic Mitchell neighborhood and at the Capitol Court Shopping Center in the Capitol Heights neighborhood.[28] For years, the department stores were known as Gimbels-Schuster's.

But unlike the common local conception, Gimbels stores did not originate in Milwaukee. At the time it acquired Schuster's, Gimbel Brothers Inc. operated fifty-three stores throughout the country, which included twenty-two Gimbels stores, twenty-seven Saks Fifth Avenue stores and four Saks Thirty-Fourth Street stores.

The founder of the department store chain was Adam Gimbel. Born in Bavaria in 1817, he immigrated to the United States in 1835. When he arrived in New Orleans, he worked for two years as a dock worker, paying close attention to the practices of itinerant peddlers who hawked their goods along the riverbanks. Gimbel purchased an inventory of needles, cloth and thread, headed north and posted listings of his goods on trees along his route. Saving his profits from this venture, he was able to purchase a horse and carriage and add to his inventory. When Gimbel arrived in Vincennes, Indiana, in 1842, he managed to sell all of his goods in one week. Soon afterward, he purchased a house that he transformed into a retail store, and he named it the "Palace of Trade." By 1887, he had opened another store in Danville, Illinois.

Hearing from his son Jacob that Milwaukee was a German stronghold, Gimbel sold his store in Vincennes, moved to Milwaukee in 1887 and negotiated the purchase of a downtown four-story store from local merchant John Plankinton. This was the first Milwaukee Gimbels.

However, Adam Gimbel and his sons were not content with their local successes. They had nationwide ambitions. Gimbel organized another store in Philadelphia. In 1910, Gimbel opened what would become a famous New York Gimbel store that would battle its archrival Macy's. Within fifteen years, it had become the largest department store chain in the nation, and by 1930, it would comprise seven flagship stores across the county, making it the largest department store conglomerate in the world.

Gimbels became even more famous for the Gimbels Thanksgiving Day parade in New York, which was founded in 1920. The parade was featured

Gimbel's downtown store in 1925. *Jeffrey Beutner collection.*

in moves such as *Miracle on 34th Street* (1947) and *Fitzwilly* (1967), and it was often mentioned as a destination of Lucy Ricardo and Ethel Mertz on the 1950s TV series *I Love Lucy*.

Back in Milwaukee, the local Gimbels was expanding in size and began carrying a variety of products. By 1923, the original store was torn down and rebuilt into an eight-story structure with escalators, restaurants and a popular walkway along the Milwaukee River.

Gimbels-Schuster's stores operated in Milwaukee until the mid-1980s. In 1973, Gimbels was acquired by Brown & Williamson, which later created the BATUS Retail Group for its retail holdings. In 1986, BATUS decided to close its Gimbels stores. The downtown Gimbels building still stands as a footprint of the past and as an anchor to today's The Avenue Shopping Mall.

STEINHAFEL'S INC.:
FOUR GENERATIONS AND COUNTING

Steinhafel's Furniture is another Milwaukee institution that was founded by Germans. Steinhafels Inc. began conducting business in 1934, when John E. Steinhafel and Arthur Mueller opened Mueller-Steinhafel Furniture at 3565 North Teutonia Avenue in today's Arlington Heights neighborhood.[29]

Mueller-Steinhafel Furniture on North Teutonia in 1940. *Steinhafel's Inc.*

John E. Steinhafel rose from humble beginnings. A grandson of German immigrants, John E. was born in Wisconsin in 1897. His father, Emil Steinhafel, worked as a cigar maker and died when John was in his teens. He and his sister were raised on North Eighth Street by their mother, Mary Schneider Steinhafel.

On completing high school, John took a job as a salesman in a furniture store, married and began a family—always keeping his mother, Mary, in the household. When John and Arthur opened the furniture store on North Teutonia, the nation was in the throes of the Great Depression. Business was likely not booming. According to the 1940 U.S. Census, John then headed a household of four children, a wife and his mother and brought in an annual income of $2,600. He reported paying $30 in monthly rent for his home.

Into and following World War II, the economy gradually improved, and the second generation of Steinhafels entered the family business. When Arthur Mueller died in 1944, the Steinhafel family bought out his share of the business. By 1959, the family had moved the furniture store to a larger location at Eighty-Fourth Street and Capitol Drive. In addition to selling retail furniture, the family started their own factory-direct mattress line called Dreams.

From that time on, Steinhafel's Inc. grew exponentially. By 2020, four generations of Steinhafels had entered the business, which, by then, included eighteen stores with over eight hundred employees in the Greater Milwaukee, Wisconsin, and Illinois area.

13.

BREWERIES

*H*ad someone been given a word association test back in the 1950s, they would likely pair the word *Milwaukee* with *beer*, then *beer* with *breweries* and *breweries* with *Germans*.

However, the first brewery in the city was not founded by Germans. It was organized in 1840 by a group of Welshmen who produced a murky, sweet, ale-flavored product that the Germans wouldn't drink. Hence, a local resident named Herman Reuthlisberger opened his own lager brewery in the Walker's Point neighborhood the following year.[30] Once the doors were opened, the Milwaukee brewing industry stormed the city. By 1856, there were over two dozen breweries in Milwaukee—all owned by and targeted to Germans. Informants from Urban Anthropology's Milwaukee ethnic study described what it meant at the local level.

> *Beer is the obvious thing. When I was a kid, there was this jingle: "I'm from Milwaukee, and I ought to know—it's draft-brewed Blatz beer, wherever you go." Sometimes it was irritating. When I'd travel and say I was from Milwaukee, all anyone would know was that it was the city with the big breweries. But you'd be hard put to find a family that didn't have someone working for the breweries. Maybe it was the breweries themselves or maybe it was the tied houses—those taverns run by the breweries. Or maybe it was advertising them or trucking the beer across the city.*

All you have to do is look around Milwaukee, to look at the good things, the nonprofit efforts of the Uihlein family, Schlitz, Pabst. It goes on and on and on, and it all came from beer.

The major brewing companies that took hold in Milwaukee were Pabst, Schlitz, Miller and Blatz. However, by today's standards, most of these began as microbreweries.

PABST BREWERY: BUSBOY TO BEER BARON

Pabst was originally named the Empire Brewery. Opened in 1842 by German immigrant Jacob Best, it established itself on "Chestnut Street Hill," near today's Juneau Avenue and Tenth Street in the Westown neighborhood.[31] When Jacob retired in 1853, his son Phillip took over and renamed Empire the Phillip Best Brewery.

Phillip Best Brewery took on the name of Pabst when a shipping captain married into the family. Johann Gottlieb Friedrich "Frederick" Pabst was born in 1836 in the Kingdom of Prussia. In 1848, he immigrated with his parents to the United States, settling in both Milwaukee and Chicago. The family was very poor. In Chicago, Frederick and his father worked as waiters and busboys. Frederick managed to get a job as a cabin-boy on a Lake Michigan steamer. He worked hard as a seaman until the age of twenty-one, when he earned a pilot's license and became captain of one of the vessels. In this capacity, he met Phillip Best. Pabst befriended the family and ended up marrying Best's daughter Maria. Following a ship accident in 1863, Pabst changed careers and purchased half of Best's brewing company.

In the meantime, Phillip Best purchased Milwaukee's first German brewery, Reuthlisberger's (later renamed Mehm's) in 1866. Best could then say that the history of his brewery went back to 1841.

By 1870, the Pabsts—Frederick, Maria and their four children—were settled in Milwaukee's Second Ward. Under Pabst's direction, the brewing company increased its beer output dramatically. He became president of the corporation in 1873, and eventually, the brewery's name was changed to Pabst Brewing Company. Construction began on a larger complex. In time, the growing Pabst family moved to an elaborate mansion at 2000 Grand Avenue (today's West Wisconsin Avenue)—a house that is still open for tours to the public.

By 1868, Pabst became the city's largest brewery; by 1874, it was America's largest brewery. In the late nineteenth century, Pabst took a blue ribbon for its brew at the Chicago beer exposition and hence named its product Pabst Blue Ribbon Beer. Soon, Frederick Pabst's influence went beyond Milwaukee and even beyond beer. Pabst controlled hotels and restaurants in New York, Minneapolis, San Francisco and Chicago, including Pabst's Loop on Coney Island and what was advertised as the largest restaurant in the world, Pabst's Harlem in Manhattan. The brewery actually hired matinee idols to visit its restaurants; they loudly proclaimed to be drinking to the health of "Milwaukee's greatest beer brewer, Captain Fred Pabst."

Prohibition took its toll on Pabst, as it did on all the city's breweries. The Eighteenth Amendment to the U.S. Constitution, which took effect in 1920 and remained enforced until it was repealed by the Twenty-First Amendment in 1933, outlawed the recreational use of alcohol. Seeing this coming, Milwaukee beer barons lobbied the U.S. Congress in an effort to

The Pabst Brewery complex, which was built at the turn of the twentieth century. The photograph was taken circa 1920. *Public domain.*

distinguish hard liquor from beer and distinguish saloons from beer gardens. They argued that the latter just constituted family outings. Their efforts were unsuccessful. During the years of national prohibition, Pabst transformed its facility to produce processed cheese. Throughout Milwaukee, taverns turned their establishments into soft drink parlors, although many, if not most, continued to sell liquor illegally.

Pabst returned to its record-setting sales in the 1930s. The brewery actually reached its apex in the 1960s and 1970s, when it advertised its beer as Milwaukee's first choice. However, change ensued. In 1985, S&P Company, based in California, purchased Pabst. The descendants of Frederick Pabst remained involved in the company but only at the periphery. Promotion of the product slowed, and Pabst faced growing competition from Miller Brewery and rising microbreweries. By 1990, Pabst was no longer profitable.

Pabst Brewery closed its doors on November 6, 1996. Over 250 skilled workers lost their jobs. The company shifted the rest of its production to Stroh Brewery in La Crosse, Wisconsin.

While the company closed down its beer production, it did not close the brewery compound. The property remained intact, awaiting future development. Within a decade, Joseph A. Zilber, a Milwaukee real estate developer and local philanthropist, purchased the complex with the plan of transforming the site into a sustainable neighborhood known simply as the

The Brew House Inn and Suites with restored copper brewing kettles, a footprint of the once-dominant Pabst Brewery. *Urban Anthropology collection.*

Brewery. Today, a remarkable footprint of the Pabst complex exists onsite. Completed in 2013, the Brewhouse Inn & Suites is now one of Milwaukee's leading hotels. It uses elements of the brewery in its décor, including restored copper brewing kettles on the second floor of the lobby and a stained-glass window depicting King Gambrinus, the folk hero of beer culture. The lobby features Jackson's Blue Ribbon Pub, which serves Pabst Blue Ribbon beer produced by Molson Coors.

JOSEPH SCHLITZ BREWING COMPANY: "BEER FOR TEDDY"

German immigrant August Krug founded a small brewery in 1849. In its first year, the microbrewery produced four hundred barrels of beer. Krug died seven years later, and his bookkeeper, another German immigrant named Joseph Schlitz, took over the business. Schlitz soon married Krug's widow, and the enterprise became known as the Joseph Schlitz Brewing Company, located in today's Schlitz Park neighborhood.[32] The microbrewery grew exponentially, and by 1869, the annual output surpassed seventy-five thousand barrels of beer.

However, Schlitz's reign did not last long. In 1875, he decided to visit his homeland. Before leaving, he took a precautionary step and wrote a will in which he left the business to the nephews of August Krug—August, Henry and Alfred Uihlein—but declared that the brewery's name could not be changed. He never came back. On the return voyage from Germany, Schlitz and 340 others perished in the wreck of the SS *Schiller* near Land's End, England.

The Uihlein brothers had been born to a family of Bavarian brewers and had arrived in America at young ages to receive an education and assist in their uncle's business. Under the leadership of August Uihlein, the Joseph Schlitz Brewing Company continued to thrive. The Uihlein family remained at the helm throughout its history.

Producing a pure product, promotion and expansion were keys to Schlitz's success. Tying the brewery to the city's growth, Schlitz developed the advertising slogan, "The beer that made Milwaukee famous." In 1902, Schlitz turned out one million barrels of beer and surpassed Pabst as the leading beer producer in the nation. When Theodore Roosevelt lead the Exposition to Eastern Africa with his son Kermit in 1909, the Schlitz brewery sent along crates of its beer, labeled, "Beer for Teddy." Nearby and not long afterward, nine bottles were found in the stomach of a dead whale.

Like Pabst, the Joseph Schlitz Brewing Company expanded its operations by purchasing corner lots in cities all over the United States. They would then build saloons on the lots where Schlitz beer would be sold exclusively. The saloons were called tied houses.

Also, like Pabst, Schlitz struggled to remain viable during national prohibition. The brewery manufactured a flavored malt syrup and chocolate bars that carried the name of Eline Candies—a strategy that helped Milwaukeeans correctly pronounce the Uihlein name. During the years of Prohibition, a growing number of African Americans were migrating north, into Milwaukee. Most settled in the Sixth Ward, where both the Pabst and Schlitz Breweries were located. However, when Prohibition ended and Schlitz once again rose to the top spot among beer producers, and despite the need for a greater workforce, both Pabst and Schlitz refused to hire Black workers for decades. At one point, William V. Kolberg, the executive secretary of the Milwaukee Urban League, and Attorney James Dorsey, the president of the NAACP, met with Milwaukee's mayor Dan Hoan and brewery heads. But during these meetings, the unions and employees blamed each other for racial exclusion, and no progress was made. As late as 1970, U.S. government civil rights investigators issued warnings to both the Schlitz and Pabst Breweries to take sufficient affirmative action in hiring Black workers and other minority workers.

By the late 1950s, Schlitz had lost its production leadership to Anheuser-Busch, but it remained securely in the second spot. During these years, the Uihlein family increased its contributions to the Milwaukee community. Not only did they own a cadre of tied houses, the exquisite Schlitz Palm Garden on Walnut Street and two Schlitz Parks—one downtown and one on the south side—but they sponsored a firework display each Fourth of July and brought the circus to town annually. The Uihleins also contributed to the construction of Milwaukee's Performing Arts Center and built the polo grounds on Good Hope Road, which has been transformed into Uihlein Soccer Park.

The brewery continued to thrive in the 1960s but faltered in the 1970s, when the company changed the beer recipe to cut operating costs. Milwaukeeans were not impressed, and sales fell. Aging facilities compounded the problem. The final blow came when the brewery's union employees walked out in a dispute over benefits and wages. The company closed in 1981.

As in the case of Pabst, beer production ceased, but the brewery itself remained intact. By 1985, a number of investors had come together with

The Old Keg House at the Joseph Schlitz Brewing Company on Rivercenter Drive, which was built in 1899. This photograph was taken the year Schlitz closed, 1981. *Alan Maganye-Roshak collection.*

a plan to revive the Schlitz complex and turn it into Schlitz Office Park. Together with city incentives, the partners invested $38 million to redevelop the site. Razing nearly twenty silos in the redevelopment, all new additions were erected to match the turn-of-the-century architecture of the old brewery. One of its major tenants became the Schlitz Brown Bottle, a café and pub that replicated the brewery's former tasting room.

VALENTIN BLATZ BREWING COMPANY: "I'M FROM MILWAUKEE, AND I OUGHT TO KNOW..."

The Valentin Blatz Brewery produced Blatz Beer at its plant at 270 East Highland in Milwaukee's East Town neighborhood until 1959, when the label was sold to Pabst Brewing Company.[33]

Valentin Blatz was born in Miltenberg, Bavaria, in 1826; there, he worked in his father's brewery as well as in breweries in Würzburg, Augsburg and Munich. With family resources, he immigrated to America and to Milwaukee between 1848 and 1849 and quickly established his own brewery. Next door was City Brewery, which had been in operation since 1846 under Johann Braun. When Johann Braun died in the early 1850s, Valentin Blatz merged both breweries, which, when combined, produced 350 barrels of lager that year. He also married Johann Braun's widow, Louisa.

Under the name of Valentin Blatz Brewing Company, the business grew rapidly. By 1868, the brewery was producing 15,366 barrels a year. By the 1880s, it ranked as the third-largest brewery in Milwaukee.

The Blatz family also grew. Living in a comfortable home on Broadway in 1880, Valentin and Louisa had four children. Valentin expanded his interests into banking and served as president of the Second Ward Savings Bank along with help from other brewer barons, including Phillip Best, William H. Jacobs and Joseph Schlitz. In 1891, Valentin Blatz sold his interests in the brewery to a group of London financiers known in brewery circles as "the English syndicate." Shortly afterward, Valentin and Louisa moved to St. Paul, Minnesota, where Val died in 1894, and Louisa died in 1907. Their bodies were returned to Milwaukee, where they were buried at the Forest Home Cemetery.

A new brewery with five stock houses was built at the Highland Avenue site in 1901. The compound was bounded by East Juneau, East Highland, North Broadway and Market Street. A Blatz office building was also erected at 1120 North Broadway—a site that occupants continued to believe was haunted over the generations.

During Prohibition, the Valentin Blatz Brewing Company adapted as creatively as Pabst and Schlitz had. Between 1920 and 1933, the brewery produced malt soap, sodas and near beer. In the decades following Prohibition, Blatz's beer production returned. It marketed its product as "Milwaukee's Finest Beer" and "Milwaukee's Favorite Premium Beer." In 1958, Pabst Brewing Company acquired Blatz, but the sale was voided the following year in violation of Section 7 of the Clayton Act as amended by the Celler-Kefauver Anti-Merger Amendment. Blatz subsequently closed, and its assets and labels were sold to Pabst.

But the Blatz beer label continued. Two popular jingles rolled out from the 1950s through the early 1970s: "Kegs, cans, or bottles, all taste the same. The three best is one beer—Blatz is the name;" and "I'm from Milwaukee, and I ought to know! It's draft-brewed Blatz beer, wherever you go."

In 1969, the G. Heileman Brewing Company acquired the Blatz label from Pabst. In an attempt to produce only beer in kegs to be served from bar taps, Heileman Blatz built a fully automated new brewery on North Tenth Street. But the effort failed, and Heileman was purchased by the Stroh Brewery in 1996. When Stroh prepared to dissolve in 1999, it sold

The building that once housed Valentin Blatz Brewery headquarters at 1120 North Broadway. *Urban Anthropology collection.*

the labels back to Pabst. The labels have since moved to the Miller Brewing Company, which became the Molson Coors Beverage Company in 2019.

But what happened to the Blatz compound? Well, that footprint of the Blatz estate remains intact. Three buildings in the German Renaissance Revival style from the Blatz plant and the Valentin Blatz Brewing Company office building got listed in the National Register of Historic Places. After being idle for nearly thirty years, the five original brewery stock houses at 270 East Highland were developed into apartments (later condos) by the Dominium Group out of Minnesota between 1983 and 1989. Called the Blatz, the current complex, with an added tower and parking structure, comprises 169 studio and one- to three-bedroom units. Amenities include common green space, central air, a sauna, an indoor pool and security.

The office building that had been the brewery headquarters was transformed, in part, to an upscale restaurant called the Beer Baron. However, in 1989, the Milwaukee School of Engineering (MSOE) purchased the land and the building in order to develop it into an alumni center. But this did not transpire without controversy. Hearing the stories

The alumni center of the Milwaukee School of Engineering, formerly the Blatz headquarters. *Urban Anthropology collection.*

that the building had been haunted by the ghost of Valentin Blatz, MSOE officials made the decision to conduct a séance. The college hired parapsychologist Carl Schuldt in 1990, paying for his consultation under their security budget. During the séance, Schuldt failed to resurrect the spirit of Blatz but did manage to rid the building of another ghost—a prickly character named Herman—who he claimed had been present at the site since 1935. The construction of the alumni center progressed without further incidence.

MILLER BREWING COMPANY: THE "HIGH LIFE"

The Miller Brewing Company was founded in 1855 by Frederick Miller. With the full name of Friedrich Eduard Johannes Müller, Miller was born in Riedlingen, Württemberg, in 1824. As a young man, he'd managed a brewery in his homeland. Miller married Josephine in Friedrichshafen, Württemberg, in 1853, and the couple had their first child the following year. The small family immigrated, with $10,000 in gold, to New York in 1854 and Milwaukee in 1855. Once settled, they faced both economic success and personal heartbreak.

Frederick Miller purchased the Plank Road Brewery at Fortieth and State Streets in today's Miller Valley neighborhood from Charles Best of the Pabst Brewing family.[34] The brewery produced three hundred barrels of beer its first year. With expansive plans, Miller began shipping beer to Chicago almost immediately, and within five years, he dispatched beer as far south as New Orleans. The Plank Road Brewery's name was changed to Miller Brewing Company, and the building compound continued to grow.

The Millers purchased a home near the brewery, where two brewers, a teamster and their families joined the Miller household. Unfortunately, personal tragedy followed. In 1860, Josephine died. Miller quickly remarried Elizabeth ("Lisette) Gross, but over the years, seven of their children failed to survive their teenage years.

By the time Frederick Miller died in 1888, the brewery was producing eighty thousand barrels of beer a year. His three living sons and son-in-law Carl took over the business. The sons introduced Miller High Life beer in 1903, and the brand immediately became popular.

As with all breweries in the United States, Miller had to adapt during Prohibition. Between 1920 and 1933, the brewery produced a cereal beverage with the "High Life" label. But despite Prohibition and the Great Depression, the Millers continued to circle its wagons and stayed viable. Miller Brewing Company remained a closed corporation well through the 1930s, with no portion of its stock ever made public. All the while, its brand continued to expand.

Change came in 1966. The brewery was then under the control of Mrs. Lorrain John Mulberger, Frederick Miller's granddaughter. She was opposed to drinking alcohol and sold the company to W.R. Grace and Company. Three years later, Grace sold the brewery to Philip Morris. Under Philip Morris, the Miller brand experienced its greatest success, rising to second place nationally after launching Miller Lite beer in 1975. The brewery continued to expand until it had brewing facilities in Chippewa Falls, Wisconsin; Trenton, Ohio; Albany, Georgia; Irwindale, California; and Milwaukee.

From that point on, a Wall Street auctioneer might have problems enumerating the changes.

- In 2001, Miller was awarded the twenty-year naming rights deal to the Milwaukee Brewers' new stadium, resulting in Miller Park.
- In 2002, Philip Morris sold Miller to South African Breweries, becoming SABMiller.

The Plank Road Brewery, circa 1870. *Molson Coors Beverage Co.*

- In 2006, Miller purchased the Steel Reserve and Sparks brands from McKenzie River Corporation.
- In 2007 and 2008, Molson Coors and SABMiller combined their U.S. operations into MillerCoors.
- In 2015, Anheuser-Busch Inbev acquired SABMiller.
- In 2016, in order to obtain the U.S. Justice Department's approval for the merger, SABMiller divested itself of its U.S. and Puerto Rican Miller brands by selling its stake in MillerCoors to Molson Coors.
- In 2019, MillerCoors changed its name to Molson Coors Beverage Company.

Tragedy struck the brewery in 2020. On February 26, at approximately 2:30 p.m., a fifty-one-year-old employee named Anthony Ferrill entered the compound and killed five other employees before committing suicide. A motive was not definitively uncovered for the mass murder.

Following the tragedy, Milwaukeeans immediately rose in support of their historic brewery. Banners and T-shirts circulated with the slogan "Miller Strong." Television stations produced segments on the brewery's winter adornments including 750,000 holiday lights and the annual Christmas tree made from hundreds of beer kegs. Taverns announced fundraisers for families of the victims. Milwaukee Brewers players at spring training pinned black ribbons to their jerseys and observed a moment of silence during a Royals game. Flowers were left outside the Molson Coors offices.

14

MACHINE SHOPS

*I*n terms of value, beer may have been Milwaukee's most important product in its early history, but by the turn of the twentieth century, the lead soon shifted to metal, turning the city into the Ruhr Valley of its time. A perfect example of the transition was the case of Falk Corporation.

FALK CORPORATION: FROM BREWERY TO MACHINE SUPER POWER

The Bavaria Brewery is one of Milwaukee's forgotten enterprises. Founded by immigrant Franz Falk in today's National Park neighborhood, it outproduced both Schlitz and Miller combined at its peak, yielding about 200,000 barrels of beer annually.[35] Born in 1823 in Miltenberg-on-the-Main, a small town in Bavaria, Franz Falk and his wife, Louisa (née Wahl), purchased a home near the Menomonee Valley, where they raised eight children.

Franz died in 1882 and left the brewery to his sons. His two oldest boys, Frank and Louis, merged Bavaria Brewery with Jung and Borchert and doubled sales. However, following two fires in three years, in 1893, the brothers sold the merged brewery to Captain Frederick Pabst of the Pabst Brewery, and the Falk beer brand gradually disappeared.

Herman Falk, the fifth of Franz and Louisa's sons, opened a machine shop of his own in 1892 in one of the vacant Bavaria Brewery buildings—now owned by Pabst. Starting out with couplings for wagons and stage equipment

Ruins of the Bavaria Brewery overlooking the Menomonee Valley. *Urban Anthropology collection.*

for the Pabst Theater, the newly created Falk Corporation developed a process to help reinforce joint connections between street rails. The company, then headquartered up the path from the original brewery in today's Menomonee Valley neighborhood, then moved into gears, creating them of all sizes to serve elevators, the gates of the Panama Canal, naval propellers of World War II battleships, moon rocket transporters and nuclear reactor cases.[36] Falk developed distributor locations and production facilities as far away as China and Australia, as well as in the United States, Mexico and Canada.

Until the recession of the 1980s, Falk Corporation enjoyed a reputation as a good company for employees. Although Falk opposed unionization, the corporation offered generous benefits to workers, including healthcare, home mortgage loans, recreational activities and college scholarships for workers' children.

Herman Falk himself had no children. He'd married Eva Wilson Wahl, a member of a wealthy Chicago family, in 1897. Eva was the niece of Herman's mother, Louisa Wahl Falk. The couple—first cousins—lived on Terrace Avenue. Eva died in 1920, and Herman died in 1947. Both were buried at the Forest Home Cemetery in Milwaukee.

Despite Herman's death, Falk Corporation remained under family direction until the late 1960s, when it lost controlling interest. The firm was then sold to Sundstrand. By the 1980s, with the global economic recession and growing European competition in the gear market, Falk's dominance began to wane. Working to improve efficiency throughout the 1990s, the company remained viable. In 2005, Rexnord Corporation, also headquartered in Milwaukee, purchased Falk for $295 million.

The following year, tragedy struck. An informant in Urban Anthropology's Old South Side oral history project described the event.

> *I was working out of my home office* [the informant lived about three miles south of the Menomonee Valley]. *I'd just gotten dressed and sat down at my desk. All of a sudden, there was a bolt of thunder like nothing I'd ever heard. The entire house shook. I ran to the front door and out to the porch. But there was nothing. Not a cloud in the sky. Nothing but sun and quiet. I came back inside and turned on the radio to see if anyone was reporting on the noise. Nothing. I called my friend who lived about a mile away. She'd heard it, too. Just the same. Her mother on the north side had called. She'd heard it, too. Finally, the radio reported that there had been this monstrous explosion at the Falk Corporation in the Menomonee Valley.*

The explosion had occurred while maintenance employees from Rexnord Falk and steamfitters from J.M. Brennan Inc. were conducting an operational test of the propane system. Gas that had been leaking from two holes in a pipe had accumulated and ignited approximately forty minutes into the test. Three workers were killed, and forty-seven other employees were injured. Following an OSHA investigation, Rexnord Falk and J.M. Brennan, the mechanical contractors, were fined for their roles in the explosion. Memorials were held across the city for the workers who'd lost their lives.

Despite the downturn in sales since the 1980s and despite the 2006 tragedy, the name Falk remains a nebula in the Menomonee Valley. The original brewery is a crumbling footprint of abandoned buildings, but Rexnord Falk still holds the reputation as "America's leading producer of industrial gear drives."

HARNISCHFEGER:
SEWING MACHINES TO OVERHEAD CRANES

Known by many names, including Harnischfeger Corporation and Harnischfeger Industries, Milwaukee's giant in mining equipment began as Pawling and Harnischfeger (P&H) in 1884. The first plant, a machine and pattern shop, was located in a two-story cream city brick building on South First Street in the Walker's Point neighborhood.[37] Following a fire in 1903, the company moved to a twenty-acre site in the Milwaukee suburb of West Milwaukee, where it would eventually become the world's leading manufacturer of overhead cranes.

The original partners at P&H were Alonzo Pawling and Henry Harnischfeger. Pawling, a pattern maker, asked Harnischfeger to purchase his share of the business in 1911, when his health declined. When Pauling died three years later, the company was renamed Harnischfeger Corporation, but it retained the P&H logo as its trademark out of respect for the cofounder.

Henry Harnischfeger had worked as a locksmith, machinist and a machine maker prior to opening his own shop. Born in Hess-Nassau in 1855, he left Germany in 1872 for New York City, where he took a job at the Singer Sewing Machine Company. Nine years later, he moved to Milwaukee and went to work for the White Hill Sewing Machine Company. There, he managed gear machining operations and castings patternmaking with Alonzo Pawling. When the company appeared to be failing, Harnischfeger and Pawling set off on their own.

Harnischfeger married Marie Hauwertz, a Wisconsin native who was sixteen years his junior. The couple resided on North Twenty-First Street, where they had two children. In 1905, they moved to a new home on Grand Avenue (today's Wisconsin Avenue) in the Historic Concordia neighborhood, which still stands today.[38] The mansion, designed by architect Eugene R. Liebert, is a fine example of the German Renaissance Revival style.

While business at Harnischfeger Corporation went through some cyclical times in its early years, the demand for cranes soared during World War I. To even out the cycles of the heavy equipment market after the war, the company's engineers designed a diverse number of construction and mining products. The firm became one of the country's largest suppliers of crawler-mounted shovels and cranes used in mining and construction by the mid-1920s. By 1930, the number of P&H employees had grown to 1,500.

The year 1930 was also when Henry Harnischfeger died. His son Walter became president. During the next two decades, Walter Harnischfeger continued to diversify production, including adding welding machinery, diesel engines and prefabricated homes to the P&H line. Despite the effort, the company was dented by the Great Depression and lost money every year from 1931 to 1939. This changed during World War II, when production was diverted to military channels. Immediately following the

The home of Marie and Henry Harnischfeger at 3424 West Wisconsin Avenue. The house remains as a footprint of the Harnischfegers' presence in Milwaukee. *Public domain.*

war, Harnischfeger Corporation responded to the housing shortage that was created by returning veterans by producing 374 prefabricated homes that were erected in Wilson Park in the Wilson Park neighborhood.

However successful the wartime years had been for P&H's bottom line, they were also when the firm's employment policies came under scrutiny. During the Great Depression, the Fair Employment Practices Committee (FEPC) had been organized by President Franklin Roosevelt under an executive order. The FEPC found systemic racism in Harnischfeger's hiring practices, including twenty-five job orders in 1941 to employment agencies that stipulated whites only. In January 1942, Harnischfeger had 3,200 employees and none of them were Black. By order of the FEPC, Harnischfeger Corporation then had to diversify more than just its product line.

Peacetime did not slow Harnischfeger's production growth. By 1953, the company employed 4,500 workers. It built new plants in Illinois, Michigan and California, and more were added and expanded in the Greater Milwaukee area. By 1976, then under the leadership of the founder's grandson—another Henry—P&H had a worldwide workforce of 8,500 and annual sales close to $800 million.

But from that time on, Harnischfeger faltered. The slide began as the market for heavy equipment relaxed. The firm lost money in 1979. The P&H payroll dropped from over 8,000 in 1970 to 3,800 in 1982, just as the recession of the 1980s rolled out. During the next two decades, amid a flurry of transactions, acquisitions (including Joy Mining Machinery), presidents not named Harnischfeger and a bankruptcy filing, Harnischfeger—then called Harnischfeger Industries—sputtered. As part of the Chapter 11 bankruptcy restructuring process in 2001, Joy Global Inc. became the direct successor to Harnischfeger Industries. In 2012, P&H Mining Equipment and Joy Mining Machinery became Joy Global. In 2017, Komatsu America Corp, a subsidiary of Komatsu Ltd., finalized an acquisition of Joy Global Inc. and added P&H and Joy to Komatsu's offerings.

Since it then owned the P&H brand, Komatsu committed in 2020 to building a new state-of-the-art facility in Milwaukee's Harbor View neighborhood.[39] This building will be less than a mile from the site of Pawling and Harnischfeger's original shop.

15.

TANNERIES

Wisconsin proved to be a first-rate state for the development of tanneries. Not only was there a steady supply of cattle from local dairy farms and meatpacking companies, but the northern counties had bountiful forests of oak and hemlock trees with thick bark that was used in tanning.

Germans arriving in Milwaukee quickly seized the opportunity. By 1860, Milwaukee had thirteen tanneries, and ten of them were owned by Germans. A decade later, the city had twenty-seven tanneries, and nineteen were owned by Germans. However, the tanneries did not merely benefit those of German descent. During Urban Anthropology's twelve-year study of Milwaukee's ethnic groups, informants were asked how their earliest Milwaukee ancestors had earned their livings in the city. The responses from Poles, Greeks, Slovenians, African Americans and Mexicans were definitive. It was not the breweries or even the machine shops that had been their major source of stable income—it was the tanneries.

PFISTER AND VOGEL: A PARTNERSHIP FOR THE AGES

Historically, the first and largest tannery in Milwaukee was Pfister and Vogel. Its principal plant operated out of the Walker's Point neighborhood.[10]

The tannery founders were Guido Pfister and Frederick Vogel, both from Württemberg. Born in Kirchheim, Württemberg, in 1823, Frederick Vogel left Germany for New York in 1846. Shortly after his move to Milwaukee, he married Auguste Juliane Herpich, who was also a German immigrant. The couple purchased a house on Fourth Street, where they raised a very large family, in which at least six children (accounts vary) lived into adulthood. The older of the partners, Guido Pfister, was born in 1818 in Hechingen, Württemberg. He emigrated in 1845. After his move to Milwaukee, Pfister married Swiss immigrant Elizabeth Gasser in 1852. The couple moved around the downtown area, eventually settling in a home on Jefferson Street. They had two children.

Pfister and Vogel arrived in New York State separately in the mid-1840s and went to work for a tannery owned by Vogel's cousin in Buffalo. They left Buffalo for Milwaukee in 1847; there, Vogel founded a tannery in the Menomonee Valley, and Pfister opened a leather retail store near today's city hall. The two men merged their interests in 1848 and formed G. Pfister & Company.

The partners' tanning business was an immediate success. By the end of its first year, production at G. Pfister & Co. comprised half of the leather market in Milwaukee. It continued to grow. Known later as Pfister & Vogel Leather Company, it was touted as the largest tannery west of the Allegheny Mountains. Pfister & Vogel's peak years were between 1880 and 1920. It opened four branches in Milwaukee by 1900, the largest of which was the Walker's Point location at the south end of the Sixth Street Viaduct. Ultimately, the company had marketing branches in Boston, New York, London, Paris, Northampton and Milan.

The number of workers continued to grow from about 500 in the mid-1880s to a workforce of over 3,500 by World War I, when it also became the world's largest tannery. The company had always welcomed new arrivals into its workforce. As African Americans began migrating from the south during these years, Pfister and Vogel became a major source of employment for the newcomers. In 1920, Pfister & Vogel agents recruited nearly 100 Mexican men to take jobs at the Walker's Point site. Known later in the Latino community as Los Primeros, the Latino migrants slept in cots in a tannery annex until they could access their own housing in the neighborhood.

However, change would follow for Pfister & Vogel. That change was the advent of the automobile. With the disappearance of horse-drawn transportation, the need for harness and buggy leather dissipated. And as the population was walking less, shoe leather was slower to wear out. Foreign leather producers also increased competition.

By 1930, the company had scaled down its tanning operations to just one plant. Military sales helped Pfister & Vogel during World War II, but production again lagged during the postwar years. The final family member to lead the company was Charles P. Vogel, the grandson of both company founders. After Vogel's death in 1959, a group of key executives purchased the operating assets from the family and ran the company until 1971. A series of owners took over the company, including Beatrice Foods, Lubar & Co., Dyson-Kissner-Moran Corp. and, finally, U.S. Leather, which produced leather for the auto industry—for a time.

U.S. Leather closed its Milwaukee enterprise in 2000, but Pfister & Vogel footprints have remained in Milwaukee. In the years just before his death, Guido Pfister, together with his son Charles, had a vision for a landmark hotel in downtown Milwaukee. They contracted with architect Charles Koch, who turned the vision into the most lavish hotel of its time in Romanesque Revival style. It had groundbreaking innovations, such as electricity and thermostat controls in every room. While Guido Pfister did not live to see its completion, Charles did. He also donated what is, today, the largest Victorian art collection of any hotel in the world. Despite rumors and purported sightings of Guido's ghost haunting the hotel's halls, the Pfister Hotel remains what is arguably Milwaukee's most distinguished hotel.

The Walker's Point complex of Pfister & Vogel shortly after it closed. *Alan Maganye-Roshak collection.*

110

However, the Pfister Hotel was not the only footprint left behind by Pfister & Vogel. Its many tannery plants have been transformed into condominiums, retail spaces and artist studios. The most notable was the Walker's Point compound, which is, today, the River Place Lofts Condominiums. The upscale complex is the only gated community near or in the downtown Milwaukee area, featuring dawn-to-dusk guarded security and total access to a boat that is available for sunset cruises, cocktail hours and other events. Individual units offer exposed timbers, cream city brick and panoramic skyline views.

TROSTEL TANNERY: TANNING BOY WONDER

Albert Gottlieb Trostel arrived in the United States and Milwaukee in late 1852, several months before his eighteenth birthday. Born into a farming family in Baden-Württemberg, he quickly embraced an interest in tanning after arriving in Milwaukee. He moved into a boardinghouse in the city's Second Ward, where he shared the dinner table with bartenders, day laborers, domestic servants, masons and a handful of the boarders' children.

Within a few years and barely out of his teens, Trostel was running his own tannery. He hired another young tanner, August Friedrich Gallun, and within months, the two pooled their efforts and founded Trostel & Gallun. The outbreak of the American Civil War in 1861 increased their production of leather goods exponentially due to the need for harnesses, saddles and boots for Union troops.

Albert Trostel married August Gallun's older sister, Charlotte Christiane Dorothea Gallun, in 1863. The couple settled in a home on Jackson Street and raised three sons and a daughter.

Despite the family connection, a schism developed at Trostel & Gallun over operating procedures, and the partners split, forming their own tanning companies with their sons. Then known as Albert Trostel & Sons, Albert Trostel's tanning business continued to grow, both in terms of productivity and building sites. The largest of the tanneries was built at 1776 North Commerce Street in today's Beerline B neighborhood in 1885.[41]

When Albert Trostel died in 1907, his sons Albert O. and Gustav took charge. The tannery reached its peak twelve years later, producing leather valued at $60 million. However, in Milwaukee and across the world, the demand for leather products was declining with the advent of the automobile in the early twentieth century. Albert Trostel & Sons

The original Trostel & Gallun tannery, circa 1880. *Marshall Street Capital.*

The Trostel Square Apartments. *Urban Anthropology collection.*

also experienced losses during the Great Depression. Under Albert O. Trostel, the company rebounded during World War II, creating leather seals and gaskets for military machinery. His son, Albert O. Trostel Jr., later assumed the helm, and the broadening of the brand continued. The company opened a new plant in Lake Geneva, Wisconsin, in the 1950s for the production of leather packings and rubber seals (later named Trostel Ltd.). During the 1960s, Albert Trostel & Sons acquired and merged with Eagle Ottawa Leather Company in Grand Haven, Michigan, maintaining the Eagle Ottawa name.

Albert O. Trostel Jr. died in 1962, and longtime executive Everett G. Smith became president of the tannery. Competition in the leather industry had grown by mid-century, with foreign producers offering lower cost imported products. Albert Trostel & Sons Co. was forced to close its Milwaukee operations in May 1969. President Everett G. Smith worked with the union to negotiate a closing agreement that was weighted heavily in favor of older workers, which included severance pay ranging from twenty-five to fifty dollars for each year of service. Over five hundred workers lost their jobs. In a company known for hiring large numbers of minorities, 60 percent of the workers were African American. Employees were offered opportunities to apply to the Grand Haven company, where positions were available.

In 1974, Everett Smith Group (ESG) was organized as a holding company for Everett Smith's interests, which included his growing ownership stake in Albert Trostel & Sons and other companies. By 2010, ESG had acquired full control of Albert Trostel & Sons and its subsidiaries Eagle Ottawa and Trostel Ltd. (which was sold in 2016). Everett Smith Group has been succeeded by Marshall Street Capital.

While the Trostel empire has disintegrated in Milwaukee, footprints remain. The plant on Commerce Street, once abandoned and briefly considered a home for a medium security prison, is now a centerpiece in a chic new neighborhood for urban sophisticates. In 2002, the Mandel Group redeveloped the site into the Trostel Square Apartments (and condominiums). The ninety-nine-unit complex has amenities that include oversized windows, private patios or balconies, a dry-cleaning service, a dog park, heated underground parking, on-site management, a fitness center and an open courtyard.

A.F. GALLUN: AND ANOTHER TANNING BOY WONDER

Born in Osterwieck-on-the-Harz, Germany, to a family of leather tanners in 1834, August Friedrich Gallun immigrated to the United States in the early 1850s, while he was still in his teens. He moved to Milwaukee and immediately went to work for Albert Trostel's Star Tannery. In just months, he became a full partner, and the pair founded Trostel & Gallun, a firm that would become known for its celebrated "blue star" harness leather.

While still with Trostel, August Gallun married Louise Christine Auguste Krause. She was also a German immigrant, and her family lived near the Granville area. The couple settled on Jackson Street, where they raised three sons and a daughter. They would later purchase a home on Prospect Avenue.

Within a decade after the Trostel-Gallun partnership was formed, the pair split and went into business with their sons. August Gallun founded A.F. Gallun & Sons, and Albert Trostel formed Albert Trostel & Sons. Gallun built his tannery in today's East Village neighborhood, near Holton and Water Streets.[42] Using some of the best architectural design of the time, Gallun's tannery gradually developed into a large complex of well-crafted buildings with easy access to water, shipping and rail lines, tanning bark and hides from nearby meatpackers. It was also a good area for an immigrant labor force. Early on, A.F. Gallun & Sons encouraged immigrants to become citizens and buy homes near the tannery. To facilitate this, the company offered them loans for home purchases. It was a good business maneuver, which ensured a stable and relatively inexpensive labor force.

The Gallun Tannery was highly successful, selling products across the United States and also in Europe and South America. In 1895, August Gallun transferred the management of the tannery to his son Albert Gallun. Under Albert's leadership, A.F. Gallun & Sons became one of the top four leather production companies in the world early in the twentieth century, at times, even surpassing Trostel and Pfister & Vogel. Specializing in products such as harnesses, boots and belts, business boomed particularly during wartime, when the need for "army leather" products for boots, rifle straps and belts increased.

Tannery business across Milwaukee generally slowed down with the development of the automobile, resulting in decreased harness use. The decline continued throughout the middle of the twentieth century. The business experienced a slight spike during the Vietnam War, when the need for boot leather once again emerged. By the late twentieth century, Gallun & Sons was having difficulty competing with the low cost of Asian leather products. The complex eventually closed in 1993, ten years after parts of Holton and Water Streets were designated as the Gallun Tannery Historic District and added to the National Register of Historic Places. At the time of its closing, 70 percent of Gallun & Sons' employees were ethnic minorities.

In 2011, a section of the tannery was razed after a wall collapsed. However, the lion's share of the compound remains as a yawning footprint of the once great tannery—it became the River House Apartments. The complex embraces four U-shaped buildings, with amenities including a swimming pool, rooftop balconies, a conference room, a resident lounge, a community room, a fully-stocked coffee station and an outdoor court for bocce ball games.

16.

EATS AND GREETS

Milwaukee has a long tradition of creating conduits for German food and drink—from breweries and cafés to bakeries, taverns, and sausage and herring shops. Many of these still operate in Milwaukee neighborhoods.

MA BAENSCH'S HERRING:
YES, "MA" REALLY DID EXIST

Known as Baensch Food Products Co. today, Ma Baensch's Herring was founded by someone who answered to the name of "Ma Baensch." Ma, or Lina, as she'd been baptized, was born in 1882 near Stettin on the Oder River. Her father and grandfather had operated a vast commercial fishery with boats and ice houses from her home north of the Baltic Sea. Lina married Otto Baensch, a textile broker, and the couple left Germany with their adult son Reinhardt to move to America in 1929. Arriving in Milwaukee, they settled in a home on Walnut Street.

Lina quickly began circulating her pickled herring in the neighborhood; it was a recipe she'd mastered back in Germany. Neighbors really enjoyed it, and within two years, she started offering her herring and other products to local stores. Despite the Great Depression, her line soared, and Ma Baensch's Herring was born in 1932. Within a few years, Lina had recruited her son Reinhardt into the business. Lina's wine sauce recipe, with thirty-two secret spices, was marketed through Boston Store, Gimbels and Schuster's.

A rendering of Ma Baensch's at Locust and Humboldt, circa 1950. *Baensch Food Products Co.*

Gradually, the Baensch line expanded to include different herring sauces and other foodstuffs, but herring remained the flagship product.

Otto Baensch died in 1937, and Ma moved in with her son Reinhardt and his new wife, Ruth, on North Forty-First Street. By 1946, Lina and her son had moved the company, then called Ma Baensch's Foods, to its current location at 1025 East Locust Street in the Riverwest neighborhood.[43] Ma, as she was called by her employees, supervised all of the pickling and packing.

However, by the 1950s, Ma Baensch had become ill. In 1951, after years of suffering, she took her own life with an automatic pistol. She was sixty-eight years old. Her son Reinhardt took over the business.

In 1999, Kim R. Wall purchased Baensch Herring. She changed the name to Baensch Food Products Co., added a gold lid and new artwork to the jars and received kosher certification to widen the customer base. However, the plant remains at its same location in Riverwest, and Ma Baensch's original herring recipe is unchanged.

Usinger's Sausage: The Epitome of Stability

Since 1880, Usinger's Sausage has been operating out of its original site on Old World Third Street (today's Martin Luther King Jr. Drive) in the Westown neighborhood.[44] As generation after generation of Usinger offspring has steered this Milwaukee institution, dozens of varieties of their Old-World sausages have achieved recognition as the best in America.

The founding patriarch, Frederick "Fritz" Usinger, was born in Wehen, Germany, in 1860. After working as an apprentice sausage maker in Frankfort, he immigrated to the United States and Milwaukee in his early twenties, with $400 in cash and a pocketful of recipes. He took a job under Mrs. Julia Gaertner in a small butcher shop on North Third Street (today's Martin Luther King Jr. Drive), and soon, he bought her out. He married Mrs. Gaertner's niece, Louise Ernestine Lorenz, in 1882, and the couple moved in above the butcher shop.

The young couple worked sixteen- to eighteen-hour days, making and selling sausage. Fritz personally delivered all his products on foot in a market basket. Most of his customers were nearby saloons whose liquor sales depended on the quality of their free lunches—hence the bar owners were willing to pay premium prices for the best-quality meats. Business grew by leaps and bounds during those early years, and the plant was enlarged and remodeled in 1909.

Fritz and Louise eventually moved into much larger quarters on West Highland Avenue, where they raised two children and employed a housekeeper and a coachman. An astute businessman and a rising associate of Milwaukee's German aristocracy, Fritz became a member of the city's most prestigious organizations, including the Masons, the Wisconsin Athletic Club, the Turnvereins, the Rotary Club and the Association of Commerce. The couple owned a summer home at Fairy Chasm, near Donges Bay, where they regularly entertained. But despite his social mobility, Fritz, like his descendants after him, never relegated company oversight to others. While the growth in business meant many more employees, Fritz Usinger insisted on keeping expansion under control so he could supervise each step of the sausage making process.

The Usinger patriarch died of a stroke in 1930, and the business was passed on to his son Fred Usinger Jr. Fred Jr. married Elsie Sophie Donges. Despite the trying times of the Great Depression and World War II, Usinger's Sausage became one of the earliest members of the Better Business Bureau during this period, an honor it still holds today.

Following Fred Jr. into leadership of Usinger's Sausage was his son, Fred Usinger III. He married Louise Ethel Dahlstrom. Like his ancestors, Fred III worked six days a week, often not leaving the premises until after 10:00 p.m. He was said to have known every one of his 150 workers (many who still spoke German) by their first names. Under Fred III, the chubby elves became a trademark of the company. He reigned over the one hundredth anniversary of Usinger's, and in 1983, he expanded the plant with an addition built on a nearby vacant parcel.

A fourth generation of Usinger descendants took over management of the company in the late 1980s. They were siblings Debra and Fritz Usinger, the great-grandchildren of the company's founder. They committed to expansion in the 1990s and opened a distribution center in Milwaukee's Walker's Point area, later moving a portion of production to a new facility next to the distribution center.

Honors would follow. A Usinger product was named the "best hotdog in the U.S." by the director of food services for the 2002 Winter Olympics, and over 700,000 hot dogs were consumed during the games. Celebrities that stopped in the shop during these times to purchase Usinger's products included Betty Ford, Liberace, Alfred Lunt and Lynne Fontanne, Shirley MacLaine and many members of the Milwaukee Brewers.

While Debra Usinger lost a battle with cancer in 2012, the responsibility of maintaining quality consistency has continued with Fritz. The original ovens and recipes remain. Modern equipment is approved only if it does not alter the taste of the sausage. Fritz Usinger, like his ancestors, oversees production of the handmade specialties from the very first stages, through smoking, packing and shipping.

Mader's: If at First You Don't Succeed…

Loosely stated, Mader's Restaurant was founded in 1902, making it the oldest eatery in Milwaukee. However, its development did not follow a straight line.

The restaurant's founder, Charles Mader, was born in Germersheim in the Rhineland-Palatinate in 1875. He left Germany for the United States in 1901. After arriving in Milwaukee, Charles was said to have taken a job as a waiter at the Schlitz Palm Garden on Third and Wisconsin Avenue. Within a year, he left his job and opened his own café on West Water Street (now Plankinton Avenue) called the Comfort. Not known for upscale cuisine, lunches at any time of day cost twenty cents, and the price included soup and a beverage of choice.

In 1904, Charles Mader married Cecilia Moedel, a German immigrant from Hungary. The couple moved frequently and had their first child the following year. But Charles apparently grew weary of the Comfort and decided to try his hand at running a new business at 270 Port Washington Road at Silver Spring Drive. The young family, then with two children (and, eventually, four), moved to that location.

The new business apparently did not suit the Maders' needs either because, by 1912, Charles had partnered up with Henry Adler, and the pair opened a saloon on Seventh and Juneau. Within a few years, Charles broke with

Adler and formed a working relationship with Gustave Trimmel, becoming a bar manager at Trimmel's saloon on North Third Street, the site of today's Mader's restaurant in the Westown neighborhood.[45] By 1918, the name had been changed to Trimmel & Mader.

The advent of Prohibition in 1920 changed the direction of the business. Trimmel had moved on, and to stay afloat without bar proceeds, Charles Mader enlisted the services of his wife, Cecilia, who had an imposing inventory of rustic German recipes, including sauerbraten, wiener schnitzel and pork shank. She became head chef. To help with expenses, Charles took on another partner, Charles Ruge, a veteran neighborhood saloonkeeper.

However, 1928 conveyed tragedy. Ruge left the business, and Cecilia Mader died. Charles then had to run the new restaurant with his sons George and Gustave. Focusing on food specialties, the family business survived until Prohibition was repealed. According to company history, Mader's served the first legal stein of beer in Milwaukee on the night of April 7, 1933.

Charles lived with his son George, his daughter Frieda and her husband and in-laws on North Fifty-Sixth Street until he died of a stroke while resting in Arkansas in 1937. The sons took over. They continued to develop the restaurant, de-emphasizing its German theme only during World War II and

Patrons at Mader's, celebrating the end of Prohibition. *Mader's Restaurant.*

the postwar years. They gradually added a new dining room, their popular boot of beer and their trademark giant pretzel. In 1950–51, the Maders hired architect William J. Ames to expand the site, creating the turreted, half-timbered face that the restaurant presents to the public today.

George Mader died in 1958, leaving Gus to run the restaurant. By 1961, Gus enrolled his son, Gustave Victor Mader "Victor," into the business. Victor added the Sunday Viennese brunch to the restaurant's offerings and created a multimillion-dollar art gallery in the lobby and upper-level areas. Victor also recruited his daughter, Kristin Mader, to manage the restaurant, bringing the generations of one family under the Mader's umbrella to four.

Von Trier: "Buzzy Got Me"

Von Trier is a tavern where the German footprint in Milwaukee neighborhoods is particularly prominent. The following quote is from an informant who discussed its significance in Urban Anthropology Inc.'s oral history of Milwaukee's lower east side neighborhood.[46]

> *I moved to the lower east side in my late teens. I thought I'd died and gone to heaven. There was the lake, the glamorous high rises on Prospect, the Oriental Theater and loads of little ethnic cafés. I remember walking by that bar that is called Von Trier today—it was called by another name. I even looked inside the door once. I wasn't old enough to drink. It wasn't until years later that I went to a movie at the Oriental with a friend, and we said, "Hey, let's go have a pint of ale at Von Trier's." We did. We went inside and then out on the patio. Everything was so gorgeous. You really had the feeling like you were in Germany—I had been there [Germany], as had my friend.*

Before the saloon was Von Trier it was Rieder's. The proprietor was Frank Rieder; he was born in 1888 in Salzbury, a town on the German–Austrian border. He; his wife, Mary (née Pernusch); and their children immigrated to the United States and Milwaukee in 1911. The German-speaking family settled on East North Avenue, near or at the site of the current Von Trier. The 1920 Census lists Frank as a baker.

In 1949, Frank Rieder erected a building that would later house the front room of today's Von Trier. He fashioned an upscale German cocktail lounge that specialized in imported beers and featured a juke box that played

Rieder's exterior, circa 1955. *Von Trier.*

only classical and European music. Several members of the Milwaukee Symphony Orchestra were regular patrons. He filled the lounge with pricey pieces of art, including a mural painted by William Lachowicz.

Frank Rieder sold his business to Karl Heinz Lotharius in 1978. A German immigrant, Karl had left his hometown at the age of twenty-four and arrived in Milwaukee in 1958. He worked multiple jobs, saved his money and first founded a downtown disco known as Oliver's in the mid-1960s—an establishment that would soon be known as "Milwaukee's busiest nightclub in town." As part of the purchase agreement with Frank Rieder, Karl was not allowed to keep the name Rieder's. Because he had been born in Trier, Rheinland-Pfalz (arguably the oldest city in Germany), Lotharius decided to retain the European ambience of the lounge and renamed it Von Trier (meaning "from Trier" in English).

Karl Lotharius was both like and unlike Frank Rieder. Like Rieder, Lotharius continued to add European art objects to the interior. This included custom-made stained-glass windows and woodcarvings from Trier.

Rieder's interior, circa 1955. *Von Trier.*

He also added the wrought-iron chandelier created by Austrian immigrant and Milwaukeean Cyril Colnik. He opened one of the city's first outdoor patios. But his personality was very different from Rieder's. While Frank Rieder was known for his sociability, Lotharius had a reputation for being demanding and confrontational, and he was particularly tough on his staff. Further complicating the issue, Lotharius was gay at a time when sexual orientation was rarely discussed. According to a 2015 Zach Brooke article in *Milwaukee Magazine*, Lotharius had a string of lovers throughout the 1970s and early 1980s, using his best friend and employee to proposition male patrons at Oliver's—young men, he thought, could be persuaded into sex with an older gentleman of means. Publicly, however, Karl angrily denied his sexual orientation.

All of this may have played a role in Lotharius's ultimate demise. Shortly after 3:00 a.m. on December 20, 1981, Lotharius left Von Trier to walk three blocks to his house on North Murray Avenue, unaware that a bowman was lying in wait. As he entered the backyard patio, he was struck in the stomach by a thirty-inch, double-barbed, razor-tipped wooden arrow. The attacker fled, and Lotharius crawled up the stairwell to the second-story flat that was occupied by his best friend and his wife. Yanking the arrow from the wound, he screamed for help.

First responders were called, but when they arrived, Lotharius was already dying from loss of blood. Slipping into shock, he cried, "Buzzy got me," to his friend and police. He died at Milwaukee County General Hospital soon afterward.

"Buzzy" was a nickname for Herbert Dolowy Jr., a one-time employee of Lotharius's downtown discotheque, Oliver's. While the full nature of Dolowy's relationship with Lotharius is not known, they did travel to Europe together in search of Old World collectibles to outfit Von Trier. Supposedly, Dolowy had been dismissed by his boss sometime prior to the killing.

Dolowy, however, had an alibi for the early morning of the murder. Milwaukee district attorney E. Michael McCann did not bring charges on the basis of the alibi and the fact that the name Buzzy was too vague. In addition, heavily redacted FBI files indicated that Lotharius had some involvement with Milwaukee organized crime, which some speculated may have played a role in his killing. The case remains open.

Following the death of Karl Lotharius, his bar manager Mark Eckert purchased Von Trier from Karl's relatives and shareholders. In 2009, Eckert sold the business to John and Cindy Sidoff, the owners of Hooligans, another popular lower east side bar. The Sidoffs continued the upscale German traditions with imported beers, as well as completing a renovation.

In 2019, Von Trier was sold to Mark Zierath of Jackson's Blue Ribbon Pub.

PART 4

Remains of German Institutions in Milwaukee Neighborhoods

17

RELIGION

*D*uring Urban Anthropology's study of Milwaukee ethnic groups, German informants discussed their ancestors' bearing on religion.

They built churches in nearly every major Milwaukee neighborhood. There is a fairly solid religious tradition, but again, assimilation just changes all that. I suspect there's probably more people of German heritage that are a part of nondenominational churches today than in some of the traditional churches.

Our religious base is substantially Catholic, and [there's] *a huge Lutheran population that comes up to almost the same size as the Catholic population....There was a huge free-thinker movement that tied in with the Socialists. And there were some Methodists and then some* [Jewish]. *Temple Emmanuel, which was on the east side here—now in River Hills—was the old German Jewish Synagogue. They brought in that tradition, too.*

While some of the German neighborhood churches, such as St. John's Lutheran and Holy Trinity (now Our Lady of Guadalupe), were central to the settlement of German Catholics and Protestants, the grandmother of them all was Old St. Mary's.

St. Mary Parish: As Old as the City Itself

St. Mary Parish (now called Old St. Mary) was built the same year that the city of Milwaukee was established—in 1846. When the earliest German Catholics began settling in the area that would become Milwaukee, many worshipped at St. Peter's at State Street and Jackson. It was an ethnically mixed parish, but as the congregation began to identify increasingly with Irish traditions, the German members moved four blocks west and built St. Mary Parish in the city's East Town neighborhood.[47]

Old St. Mary's Church at 844 North Broadway, circa 1880. *Milwaukee Archdiocese.*

Among the prime movers in the establishment of St. Mary's were Bavarian mission societies and the St. Anne Women's Society. The women's society raised funds through bazaars, bake sales and other efforts to finance the new church.

St. Mary Parish was designed by architect Victor Schulte. In 1848, King Ludwig I of Bavaria gave the parish a painting that depicts the Annunciation; it was purportedly crafted by Munich court artist Franz Xaver Glink. The work was hung above the high altar. According to the parish's website, "The *Stations of the Cross*, also painted in Munich, was the gift of the parish Saint John Young Men's Sodality." The church's first pastor was Bavarian-born Father Michael Heiss, who later became the second archbishop of Milwaukee.

St. Mary's never completely lost its German congregation. However, as the generations passed, members of other ethnic groups also began to call the parish their home. Most prominent were the Puerto Ricans. Arriving in Milwaukee a century after St. Mary's was built, the Puerto Ricans settled in an area just northeast of downtown that was bounded roughly by Milwaukee, Van Buren, State and Lyon Streets in the Yankee Hill neighborhood.

The newcomers made St. Mary's their church. This lasted until the early 1960s, when the City of Milwaukee began implementing urban renewal plans, which called for the demolition of most of the properties in the Puerto Rican neighborhood. The Puerto Ricans were forced to leave the area they had settled, many compelled to sell their homes for half of what they'd paid for them—if they were offered funds at all. Most gradually migrated into the Riverwest neighborhood.

Today, Old Saint Mary Parish is listed in the National Register of Historic Places.

St. Francis de Sales Seminary: Preserving Everything German…For a Time

As German Catholics became more numerous in Milwaukee in the mid-nineteenth century, one man took notice—John Martin Henni. Born to a German-speaking family in Switzerland in 1805, he went to Rome in 1824 to advance his studies in philosophy and theology. A few years later, he received an invitation from Bishop Edward Fenwick to join the Diocese of Cincinnati in the United States. Henni answered the call and was later ordained to the priesthood by Fenwick. While in Ohio, Henni became interested in religious

St. Francis de Sales Seminary, located in the Milwaukee suburb of St. Francis, on the border of Milwaukee's Fernwood neighborhood, circa 1970. *Alan Maganye-Roshak collection.*

leadership to Germans in the United States. He proposed a seminary for the education of priests to minister among German Catholics.

This mission was advanced when Henni was appointed to the newly created Diocese of Milwaukee by Pope Gregory XVI. In 1843, Henni organized the St. Francis de Sales Seminary in his Milwaukee residence. He and other members of the newly formed Archdiocese soon saw the need for a larger site for the seminary. In 1853, a papal envoy accompanied the bishop to an area on the border of today's Fernwood neighborhood.[48] Lore says that the envoy, overcome by the site's beauty, shouted, "Make this place holy!" By January 1856, a new building, designed by Victor Schulte (the same architect of Old St. Mary Parish), was dedicated on the feast day of St. Francis de Sales.

Archbishop Henni and his successors, Archbishops Michael Heiss and Frederick Xavier Katzer, engraved a resilient German character on the new jurisdiction. This "Germanization" policy was continued but to a lesser extent by Archbishop Sebastian Messmer. Strongly believing in the adage "language preserves faith," the local German Catholics strove to maintain a more or less homogeneous religious community, in which German language and ethnic traditions would be preserved. This became a practice that was most strongly reproduced in the Diocese of Milwaukee with the establishment of German-speaking parishes and schools. For many years, St. Francis Seminary specialized in the education of German-speaking youth for service to German Catholics in the Midwest and beyond.

Not everyone was pleased with the German domination of the diocese. Conflicts between German and non-German clergy (particularly the Irish) erupted. Some demanded English-speaking clergy. Germans shunned cultural assimilation, insisting that their schools and religious life remain distinct, and they continued to request German-speaking bishops to minister to their needs.

But by the late nineteenth century, the German hold on Milwaukee began to weaken. In the 1880s, the shift of the local economy to heavy industry brought a large influx of Southern and Eastern European Catholics to the city, resulting in a more diverse Catholic population. Bohemians, Italians and Poles were arriving and establishing their own Catholic parishes.

Despite the tension, the seminary remained strong. In 1868 and 1875, additions were made to the original building, and enrolment grew. Eventually, the St. Francis de Sales Seminary would also offer graduate degree programs for lay candidates. The seminary remains strong today.

18.

SCHOOLS

A German informant from Urban Anthropology's ethnic study underscored the role of German women in establishing Milwaukee educational institutions.

There is a strong emphasis that the Germans picked up from the Yankees but ran with the ball—so to speak—in educational development, including working to create colleges and universities. Concordia College is one thing. But Alverno College is a result of German Catholic nuns. Mount Mary College, Stritch College—German-women, religious-producing colleges.

MOUNT MARY UNIVERSITY AND THE SCHOOL SISTERS OF NOTRE DAME

A massive Gothic convent with fairytale gardens and stone grottos once adorned the intersection of Milwaukee and Ogden Streets. The convent, at one time showcased on photograph postcards, was home to the School Sisters of Notre Dame, first organized by Mother Caroline Friess of Bavaria. At its peak, the jurisdiction instructed students in 147 Wisconsin schools, including today's Notre Dame Middle School and Messmer High School.

While the site was demolished at the close of the 1950s, when the convent moved to Mequon, Wisconsin, footprints of the work of the School Sisters remain in Milwaukee. Today's Mount Mary University in the Mount Mary

Above: The convent of the School Sisters of Notre Dame, circa 1890. *Milwaukee County Historical Society.*

Left: An architectural drawing of Messmer High School, which was built in 1929 on West Capitol Drive. This drawing was created circa 1928. *Messmer High School.*

An aerial view of Mount Mary on North Menomonee River Parkway in the 1930s. *School Sisters of Notre Dame.*

neighborhood was the result of the work of the School Sisters of Notre Dame.[49] Founded in 1913 in Prairie du Chien, the School Sisters established St. Mary's Institute, introduced a college curriculum, received a charter from the State of Wisconsin and opened the state's first four-year, degree-granting Catholic college for women. They moved St. Mary's to Milwaukee, renamed it Mount Mary and opened the doors to students in 1929.

In 2013, Mount Mary became Mount Mary University. With nearly 1,500 students today, the university offers more than thirty academic majors, as well as eight master's and doctoral degree programs.

Alverno College and the School Sisters of St. Francis

Another German religious community left its imprint on Milwaukee educational institutions—the School Sisters of St. Francis, which was founded in 1874. When the community had grown to ten members, the sisters left Germany for America with the mission of helping new immigrants. Settling first in New Cassel, Wisconsin, they soon built a new motherhouse in Milwaukee on Twenty-Seventh (today's Layton Boulevard) and Greenfield—which, at the time, was at the edge of the city. The newly established St. Joseph Convent organized a school with the sprawling name of St. Joseph's Academy and High School for Girls and Young Ladies. By 1920, the academy had added a two-year, post-secondary program and renamed itself St. Joseph Normal School. Then, in the 1930s, the normal school morphed into a four-year institution under the title of Alverno Teachers' College. The School Sisters expanded the college to a fifty-acre site in today's Alverno neighborhood—an area that was, once again, at Milwaukee's edge.[50]

Both St. Joseph Convent and Alverno still stand today. By the 1950s, the name of Alverno Teachers' College had been changed to Alverno College. Its original buildings included the main administration structure (now Founders' Hall) and its classrooms, chapel, cafeteria and kitchen; the auditorium and gym to the south; and Corona Hall (dormitory) to the north. By 1956, the resident population had outgrown Corona Hall, and the construction of Clare Hall was begun. In the 1960s, Loretta Hall (now Austin) and the Nursing Education Building were added. In the 1970s, Weekend College (now known as Alverno on the Weekend) was launched to reach out to working women who lacked the time to earn their degrees. Over one thousand students commute daily to the campus.

CARDINAL STRITCH UNIVERSITY AND THE SISTERS OF ST. FRANCIS OF ASSISI

Yet another Milwaukee college that was developed by German Catholic nuns was Cardinal Stritch. Founded in 1937 by the Sisters of St. Francis of Assisi as St. Clare College, the function of the south side institution was to train female teachers. It was renamed Cardinal Stritch College in 1946 in honor of Milwaukee's Cardinal Samuel Stritch. After opening its doors to men in 1956, the college gradually expanded to include a large variety of majors and a graduate school.

Cardinal Stritch left its south side location in 1962 and relocated to a roomier spot in Milwaukee's northern suburb of Fox Point. However, beginning in 2009, the institution moved its College of Education and Leadership to Milwaukee's Westown neighborhood at Tenth Street and McKinley Avenue in buildings that were once part of the Pabst Brewery complex.[51]

The college was renamed Cardinal Stritch University in 1997. Today's university includes programs in health sciences, English, art, preprofessional studies, psychology, sociology, religion and philosophy, criminal justice, communication, business, history and pollical science, mathematics, natural sciences, Spanish, theater, computer science and music, as well as education.

In 2017, the Milwaukee buildings were sold to a developer that, at the time of this writing, is converting them into a high-end residential complex.

Concordia University and the Lutheran Church–Missouri Synod

Authorized by the Lutheran Church–Missouri Synod, Concordia's original 1881 site was a basement in Trinity Lutheran Church in downtown Milwaukee. Its inaugural class was composed of thirteen students. A year later, the college moved to Thirty-First Street, between State and Highland, in a neighborhood that would later be designated, appropriately, Historic Concordia.[52]

Concordia College (as it was originally named) remained at that site until 1983; it initially offered high school classes and the first two years of a liberal arts program. It later became a four-year accredited college. In its early years, most of Concordia's students were German-speaking farm boys from states in the Midwest. In the 1960s and 1970s, the college incorporated a lay ministry program and coeducational components for those interested in becoming deaconesses, teachers or social workers in the Lutheran Church. Concordia also added business and secretarial courses to its curriculum.

For the century that the college remained in the neighborhood, it was the area's anchor and chief developer, routinely purchasing available homes to house its students. Concordia also purchased some homes for their land value, keeping them only for future expansion possibilities. But in 1982, the Lutheran Church–Missouri Synod purchased a large parcel of land in the northern Milwaukee suburb of Mequon that was owned by the School Sisters of Notre Dame. Concordia left the neighborhood for the larger site a year later; there, it eventually became Concordia University. During Urban Anthropology's oral history of the Historic Concordia neighborhood, residents lamented the move.

> *For years, we fought to get the college to take care of these houses it bought and then just left to rot. But we thought they were going to expand in our neighborhood and we could work with them. But no—they decided to leave the neighborhood altogether.*

The very name of the neighborhood was named after Concordia College. Concordia College, after investing in the neighborhood and plowing down a bunch of houses, picked up and moved up to Mequon. Those were huge changes.

Residents, however, spoke very highly of the later developments that were initiated by the Forest County Potawatomi. The Potawatomi, who operate the Potawatomi Hotel and Casino in Milwaukee's Menomonee Valley, purchased the Concordia buildings in 1990 and have since been engaged in restoring both the college halls and some of the decaying houses, ensuring that Concordia's footprints remain in the neighborhood. Now called the Wygema Campus, the college halls currently function as school and office space for the tribe and others. In addition, a strip of duplexes has been renovated and converted into habitable rental properties.

MILWAUKEE SCHOOL OF ENGINEERING: SPRINTING AHEAD ON TECHNOLOGY

Founded in 1903 in response to the growing local needs for workers in technical fields, today's Milwaukee School of Engineering (MSOE) is spread across twenty-two acres in Milwaukee's East Town neighborhood.[53]

Its beginnings were unpretentious. School founder Oscar Werwath, an immigrant from Saxony, Germany, was a practicing engineer who'd graduated from European technical schools. He was only twenty-three years old and had just arrived in America when he began organizing the school—originally called the School of Engineering of Milwaukee. Working with business and industry leaders in the city, Werwath and his partners' goals were to prepare men and women to fill newly created technical positions. The first specializations they developed were electrical engineering, radio, welding, refrigeration, heating and air conditioning. After a short residence at Rheude's Business College, the school moved to a modest building on Winnebago Street, where it graduated its first class. In 1911, the school relocated to the Stroh building, just a few blocks south of downtown Milwaukee.

The student body and the programs at MSOE expanded over the decades in response to local and national needs. In 1935, the school's board established the Industrial Research Institute, where students and faculty could collaborate with local industries for work. The school purchased the

The original location of the School of Engineering of Milwaukee on Winnebago Street, circa 1906. *Milwaukee School of Engineering Archives.*

German-English Academy building for the function. Another example of the school's response to local needs occurred on the eve of World War II, when the school partnered with the National Youth Administration, Catholic Youth Organization, University of Wisconsin Extension and the YMCA to develop and offer aerial training opportunities. By 1940, the Greater Milwaukee area had 250 licensed pilots.

Today, located on its East Town campus, MSOE attracts students from all areas in the United States and across the globe. It offers fifteen bachelor's and ten master's degree programs.

19

HEALTHCARE

*T*he following is a quote from a German informant in Urban Anthropology's twelve-year Milwaukee ethnic study who summarized German healthcare attitudes, practices and contributions.

> *The original Germans were a little leery of vaccinations. They lost a lot of children. But in general purposes, they are a very clean people. Clean in their houses—meticulously clean in their houses—clean in their yards, careful of disposal of waste. And German religious sisters started hospitals. Lutheran Hospital in Milwaukee, which has been put out of business by Mount Sinai [Samaritan], was a German Lutheran hospital. St. Michaels is another one. St. Joseph's Hospital—they [sic] were started by Catholic nuns. So, they were, in that sense, very progressive. Germans also took care of the elderly and children. Of their own denominations, however.*

Among the major healthcare institutions founded by early Milwaukee Germans are Lutheran, Deaconess, St. Michael's and St. Joseph's Hospitals.

LUTHERAN AND DEACONESS HOSPITALS: SPIRITUAL HEALTHCARE TO SPIRITUAL NEIGHBORHOOD CARE

First named Milwaukee Hospital, Lutheran Hospital was founded in 1863 by William Passavant, a Pittsburgh pastor and son of German immigrants. Milwaukee Hospital was preceded in the city only by St. John's Infirmary, which later became St. Mary's Hospital. The impetus for Passavant's work was the cholera pandemic of 1846–60.

Initially called "the Passavant," the original care facility was organized in a converted farmhouse. By the 1880s, a new structure had been built at Twenty-Second and Kilbourn Avenue in the city's Avenues West neighborhood.[54] The sisters of the deaconess order provided care. Patients who were receiving healthcare for free were expected to work for the hospital to pay off their debts after recovery.

The facility was renamed Lutheran Hospital in 1966 and went on to add a four-hundred-bed patient tower in 1973. Due to changes in healthcare financing, neighborhood demographics and medical technology, mergers followed. In 1980, Lutheran Hospital merged with Deaconess Hospital (founded by German sisters in 1909) to form Good Samaritan Medical Center; and in 1987, Good Samaritan and Mount Sinai Hospitals merged to form Sinai Samaritan in partnership with Aurora Health Care. Two campuses operated for a time. Good Samaritan continued at the Kilbourn location and Mt. Sinai on North Twelfth Street. By 1996, the Kilbourn location was closed.

But footprints of Lutheran Hospital remained. In 2000, Aurora Healthcare transferred four of the Kilbourn buildings, totaling 321,000 square feet, to a newly incorporated, faith-based nonprofit, City on the Hill. Since then, the organization has used the campus to promote neighborhood health through a wide range of youth and family programs and the development of 150 units of affordable housing for families and senior citizens.

St. Joseph and St. Michael Hospitals
and the Wheaton Franciscans

The Wheaton Franciscans—originally the Congregation of Franciscan Sisters, Daughters of the Sacred Hearts of Jesus and Mary—was founded by Mother M. Clara Pfaender in Olpe, Germany. Partnering with Bishop Conrad Martin of the diocese of Paderborn, Germany, Sister Pfaender envisioned a Franciscan community of women who were dedicated to prayer, teaching, healing and the care of orphans. The congregation moved to the United States and St. Louis, where the sisters began establishing American hospitals. Two of these hospitals were in Milwaukee.

St. Joseph Hospital was founded in a little house on Walnut Street in the late 1870s by the Franciscan Sisters. By the 1880s, its patient load had

St. Michael Hospital, circa the late 1950s. *Karl Bandow collection.*

outgrown the facility. Together, with the nuns, city leaders raised $30,000 to build a forty-bed facility at North Fourth and West Reservoir Streets. This served Milwaukee's near north side for nearly fifty years. Needing more space in 1930, St. Joseph Hospital was moved to a new campus in the Sherman Park region, in a neighborhood that would eventually be named in its honor—the St. Joseph neighborhood—at 5000 West Chambers Street.[55]

The old facility on North Fourth and Reservoir did not remain vacant for long. Although the (Wheaton) Franciscan Sisters had initially sold the property, they repurchased it in 1937, renovated the facility and renamed it St. Michael Hospital. St. Michael's remained at this location for nearly twenty years. In 1957, the hospital was relocated to 2400 West Villard Avenue in Milwaukee's Lincoln Park neighborhood.[56] However, by the turn of the twenty-first century, the hospital was struggling with a dwindling patient count and financial losses. It closed in 2006 and moved the majority of its services to St. Joseph Hospital.

St. Joseph—now Ascension SE Wisconsin Hospital–St. Joseph Campus—is the remaining footprint of the two healthcare facilities. It is the only hospital serving the predominantly African American neighborhoods between downtown and the Milwaukee suburb of Wauwatosa.

PART 5

Remains of German Ways of Life in Milwaukee Neighborhoods

20.

SOCIAL/RECREATIONAL

*A*s with Milwaukee commerce, much of the German influence on the city's social and recreational life was related to beer. In the following quote, an informant in Urban Anthropology's Milwaukee ethnic study summarized the point.

> *Milwaukee's park system rivals none. But it all started with the German beer gardens. And from that, you had Whitnall and some of the Germans in Milwaukee's Socialist movement that laid out a network of parks all over the county. Now, it's a full circle with beer gardens coming back.*

LUEDDEMANN'S-ON-THE-LAKE: FORERUNNER OF THE GERMAN BEER GARDENS

It all started with the German-born family of Gustav Lueddemann. Immigrants from Saxony, Gustav and Gertrude Lueddemann and their children came to the area that would become Milwaukee and purchased a tract of land on the shores of Lake Michigan in the 1830s. During this time, Native tribal lands were being surveyed by the U.S. government and subsequently sold to White settlers. Unlike many other early Wisconsin landowners, the Lueddemanns did not clear their tract for timber production. Farming one section, they left most of the forest intact.

A painting of Lueddemann's farm by Franz Hölzlhuber (1826–1898). *Wisconsin Historical Society, WHS-043566.*

By 1850, the Lueddemanns had turned their home into a picnic area and a farm-to-table restaurant. Milwaukeeans travelled by foot, wagon or boat on Sundays to enjoy the best beer, wine, butter, cheese and bacon the family had to offer. Concerts were also held at what had become known as "Lueddemann's-on-the-Lake."

Following Gertrude's death, the family sold the land to the Milwaukee Park Commission, which had been organized the previous year. The Lueddemann tract ultimately became the northern section of the Lake Park neighborhood.[57] At the time, Christian Wahl, another German Milwaukeean, was president of the commission and sought to utilize the Lueddemanns' site to increase Milwaukeeans' access to Lake Michigan. He sought the help of the noted Central Park landscape architect, Frederick Law Olmsted. Olmsted's firm ultimately took over the design process. Maintaining many of the features of the Lueddemann property, Olmsted added some of his signature elements, such as fountains, ravines and ornate bridges. Today, an ice rink warming house stands on the very site of the old Lueddemann farmhouse.

THE SCHLITZ BEER GARDENS: NOT YOUR EVERYDAY PICNIC GROUNDS

Following the Lueddemanns' lead, the breweries began purchasing tracts of land, and on them, they would build what later became known as beer gardens. By the 1880s, Milwaukee's park area consisted of a meager seven acres that were owned by the city along the lake bluff, thirty acres at the north side reservoir, two and a half acres that comprised George Walker Square on the south side and a triangle with a horse trough and fountain at Mitchell Street and Kinnickinnic Avenue. Beer gardens would change all of that. The leader in this pursuit was the Joseph Schlitz Brewing Company. While Schlitz built the Palm Garden downtown, on the corner of Third and Wisconsin, arguably, the two most spectacular beer gardens were in Milwaukee's outlying neighborhoods of the time—one on the north side and one on the south side.

In 1879, Schlitz purchased privately owned picnic grounds; they were previously owned by Prussian immigrant Charles Quentin. The tract was located on Eighth Street, between Walnut and Brown, in today's Hillside neighborhood.[58] On the seven acres, there was a forty-foot-tall hill that the brewery fashioned into the centerpiece of what would become Schlitz Park, adding a three-story lookout pagoda. The fully developed beer garden could accommodate twenty thousand individuals at any given time. Its features included a hotel at the park's entrance, a zoo to the right of the entrance, a concert pavilion, a bowling alley, a winter dance hall and a refreshment parlor. Sunday programs at Schlitz Park ranged from diving horses to operas that featured performances of Verdi, Mozart, Wagner and Gounod in the summer.

On the south side, Schlitz opened another beer garden at the turn of the twentieth century. It was called the Schlitz Tivoli Palm Garden, and it was located on National Avenue in the Walker's Point neighborhood.[59] As lavish as Schlitz Park was, the Trivoli Palm Garden featured a thirty-foot-tall domed ceiling, gilding, hand carvings, Bedford stone trimmings, cathedral glass, murals depicting tropical paradises and enormous potted palms throughout the site. Also equipped with a large seating capacity, the beer garden became a gathering place for the city's most influential citizens. The Arthur Pryor and Bohumir Kryl bands were featured there regularly.

While the minority Yankee population in Milwaukee called the beer gardens "Sunday orgies," their continental appearance and amenities were a major attraction for Germans and other European immigrant groups. During their heyday, they appealed to families and patrons of all age ranges.

The entrance to Schlitz Park with the pagoda in background, circa the 1890s. *Milwaukee Public Library, Remember When Collection, RW 627.*

However, the beer gardens had dwindled by the 1920s. A combination of factors played roles in their demise, including anti-German sentiment during World War I, the advent of national prohibition and the organization of a city park commission that developed parks with free access. Nevertheless, footprints of the Schlitz neighborhood beer gardens remain. Schlitz Garden later became a Milwaukee County park named Carver, after George Washington Carver. The building that housed the Trivoli Palm Garden remains today. Following a devastating fire in 1969, the City of Milwaukee moved to condemn and raze the burned-out shell, but a Historic Walker's Point preservation group stepped in to save it. Today, it is occupied by a new initiator of city social life—the nonprofit NEWaukee. This social architecture firm hosts the Wisconsin Avenue Night Market, Urban Island Beach Party and a number of other popular city events.

SCHUETZEN PARK: FROM SHOOTING RANGE TO CARNIVAL SITE TO COUNTY PARK

In 1866, a German club called the Milwaukee Schuetzen purchased several acres of land between North Third (now Martin Luther King Drive) and North Fifth Streets, just south of West Burleigh in today's Harambee neighborhood.[60] They used the tract as a shooting range and gradually added a beer garden, saloon, bowling alley and dance hall.

In the 1890s, Captain Frederick Pabst of the Pabst Brewing Company purchased the land. He kept the beer garden but transformed the shooting range area into a carnival ground with a miniature railroad, a funhouse called Katzenjammer Castle and a figure-eight roller coaster. The site drew thousands of patrons during warm-weather months. But when national prohibition was rolled out in 1920, Milwaukee was forced to close its beer gardens, including this one. Pabst sold the tract to Milwaukee County.

Milwaukee County redeveloped the site into Garfield Park, named after President James A. Garfield. In 1982, the park was renamed Rose Park after longtime county supervisor "Homer" Clinton Rose. Today, the Clinton Rose Senior Center sits at the corner of Rose Park.

COLD SPRING: FROM RACE TRACK TO NEIGHBORHOOD

Milwaukee's Cold Spring Park neighborhood's first wave of residents weren't American Natives, Yankees or Germans—they were Saddlebreds, Hackneys and Standardbreds.[61] Today's neighborhood is the remaining footprint of a famous (some would say, infamous) racecourse.

A year after the city of Milwaukee was formed in 1846, well-heeled residents—most with trolling rigs—decided they should have a place to race their horses. Having scouted out various locations, a group decided to race on the Cold Spring Farm off the western edge of the developing city. They purchased the farm and paid to have the land ploughed and fashioned into a twenty-foot-wide, one-mile-long racetrack called the Cold Spring Racing Course. A second half-mile track, stables, maintenance buildings and the Cold Spring Hotel were also constructed there. Milwaukee's Germans were involved at every level of development, from investments, to management, to actual racing.

However, the race track and hotel did not enjoy the best of reputations. Race contestants bet heavily, many drank to excess and the hotel became known as a place for cockfighting and courtesans.

The racecourse was closed briefly during the Civil War, when it became Camp Washburn, a training camp for Wisconsin soldiers. Following the war, the buildings that had been used for barracks, officers' quarters and a hospital during the conflict were turned into stables and outbuildings for up to 150 horses. In 1871, a world record was broken at the Cold Spring track when the mare Goldsmith Maid trotted a mile in two minutes and seventeen seconds. As the years passed, other events were added to the course, including boxing matches, conventions, weddings, circuses and bicycle races.

Racing competitions were often fierce between European and American contestants at the track. Fans were particularly pleased when those who prevailed were not just Americans but Milwaukeeans as well. In this climate, two local German Americans—one amateur and one professional—became national cycling stars at the Cold Spring track at the end of the nineteenth century. Con Reinke, who'd arrived from Germany in 1881 and lived in Milwaukee's Ward 15, broke a world amateur cycling record at Cold Spring in 1896. Henry Kanaska, who lived with his parents on Cedar (today's Kilbourn Avenue), was born in America, but only five years after his father arrived from Germany. He was ranked among the top indoor professional track riders in America in the 1890s and was a regular contestant at Cold Spring.

By the turn of the twentieth century, the surrounding streets were filling in with residents and butting up against the track. The Cold Spring Race Course was ultimately subdivided into lots and later became the Cold Spring Park neighborhood.

21

ARTS/CULTURAL

*I*t would be difficult to overstate the German influence on Milwaukee's cultural landscape. The following quotes are from informants in Urban Anthropology's twelve-year Milwaukee ethnic study. In them, they discuss Germans and theater.

And that area [Milwaukee's current theater district] *was really settled early by the Germans because it was on the east side of the river, and it was the least attractive place because it was wet. Very wet.*

You can't go anywhere in Milwaukee without seeing the influence of Germans in art. They founded the theaters. They owned them. They built them. An old German told me his grandfather had said that they needed to live up to [Milwaukee] *being called the German Athens.*

And the Melody Top came out of that German theatrical tradition. Everyone I knew went there. It opened up when I graduated from high school, and it was a great date place to go. The plays were super. You had major movie and stage stars performing there. My boss once saw Jane Powell in a production. We went there when it was just a tent.

PLAYHOUSES: "THE FINEST IN THE COUNTRY"

In 1868, the Kurz family built the Stadt Theater in Market Hall, where the Milwaukee City Hall now resides. They soon moved the facility to North Third Street, near Walnut, where they opened with a one-thousand-seat capacity. Its German stock company produced classical German drama and was considered the pride of Milwaukee's Teutonic culture.

However, complaints began to air in the media that Milwaukee, called the German Athens of America, had no "temple of music." Responding to this complaint in 1871 was a butcher with a background in theater named Jacob Nunnemacher, who founded Nunnemacher's Grand Opera House. Known locally as "the Nunnemacher," the opera house was built on East Wells Street in the city's East Town neighborhood.[62] The Stadt Theater closed in 1890, and shortly afterward, beer baron Captain Frederick Pabst purchased the Nunnemacher, hoping to combine the traditions of the Stadt with those of the opera house. He closed the theater for remodeling, hoping to reopen it with the name *Das Neue Deutsche Stadt-Theater* (the New German Theater). Just before the reopening, a fire destroyed the building. Pabst instantly ordered the theater to be rebuilt—this time, with the name of Pabst Theater.

Under Pabst's direction, the new theater, designed by noted architect Otto Strack, was rebuilt in less than a year. It reopened to crowds in November 1895. A New York City critic called the Pabst Theater "the finest in the country," surpassing anything to be found in New York, Philadelphia, Chicago or Boston. The theater became home to German repertory and stock companies, with most productions being performed in German until the 1920s. Today, the highly acclaimed Pabst Theater remains at its original downtown address at 133 East Wells Street.

However, not all playhouses in the German tradition were located downtown. One of the best examples of a playhouse in Milwaukee's outlying area was the Melody Top Theater. Opened in 1963, the Melody Top was originally an outdoor tent theater. It was built in today's Brynwood neighborhood in Milwaukee's Granville area—then a heavily German region.[63] The theater would soon replace the tent with a wooden dome and featured a mixture of popular musicals and classic operettas, usually with a star performer, such as Chita Rivera, Van Johnson or Christine Ebersole. The theater closed when its main backer, William Luff, died in 1987.

MOVIE THEATERS: DEVELOPERS AND ARCHITECTS

Local Germans did not limit themselves to live theater. While the Irish Saxe brothers, John and Tom of Saxe Amusement Enterprises, may have operated the first chain of theaters in the Milwaukee area, two architectural firms with German leadership and two German Jewish developers played key roles in the city's first wave of movie theaters.

Gustave A. Dick and Alex Bauer, partners in the Dick and Bauer Architectural Firm, were both sons of German immigrants. Their firm designed sixteen movie theaters in and around Milwaukee. The most lavish of these were the movie palaces—the Oriental and the Tower. The Tower, which opened in 1926 on North Twenty-Seventh Street, featured elegant Spanish and Mediterranean themes. The Oriental, which opened the following year on North Farwell, was designed with East Indian elements, including two minaret towers, eight porcelain lions, six larger-than-life Buddhas and hundreds of elephants.

Another architectural partnership, Charles Kirchoff and Thomas Rose, designed a host of early theaters. The senior partner, Charles Kirchoff, was the son of German immigrants. Rose was Irish. Included among the local theaters they designed were the American, Colonial, Crystal, Garden, Majestic, New Star, Palace, Rialto, Riverside and Star. The Palace and Riverside were the most opulent. The Palace, which opened in 1916 on West Wisconsin Avenue, seated 2,437 on its main floor, and it had a balcony with boxes that had 20 seats each. The Riverside, which opened in 1928, also on West Wisconsin Avenue, seated 2,558 on its orchestra level and had three boxes on each wall.

Two real estate developers who were deeply involved with the early wave of movie theaters were Moses Annenberg and Oscar Brachmann, both sons of German Jewish immigrants. Moses Annenberg operated M.L.A. Investment Co., which purchased both the Tower and Oriental Theaters from Saxe Amusement Enterprises as part of a selloff that preceded the sale of the entire company in the late 1920s. Oscar "Marc" Brachman, the developer of Milwaukee's Astor Hotel, also built movie theaters. One of the theaters was the Rialto, which was built in 1921 with architects Kirchoff and Rose; and another was the Downer, which was built in 1915 with Swedish architect Martin Tullgren. Brachman partnered with the Saxe brothers in the building of the Downer Theater.

The Oriental Theater in 1931. *Milwaukee Public Library, Remember When Collection, RW2156.*

Today, the Downer, which is still standing in Milwaukee's Murray Hill neighborhood, is the city's oldest movie theater that continues to show films.[64] The Riverside, in the Westown neighborhood, has been transformed into an opulent concert hall.[65] The Oriental, with its signature minaret towers, remains as the iconic symbol for Milwaukee's lower east side.[66]

PUBLIC ART: SCULPTURE TO STAND

Nearly all the major examples of public art created by Germans in Milwaukee's developing years still adorn the city's neighborhoods. These include the *Spirit of Commerce* statue in Jackson Park, designed by Gustave Haug in 1881; the Lion Bridges in Lake Park, designed by Oscar Sanne in 1896; the *Eight Stone Lions* in Lake Park, designed by Paul Kupper in 1897; the *Carnival Column* on Wisconsin Avenue, designed by Alfred C. Clas in 1900; the monument of Erastus B. Wolcott in Lake Park, designed by Francis Herman Packer in 1920; the *Fishing* statue in the Parklawn Housing Project, designed by Karl Kahlich in 1938; and *Bird and Fish* at the headquarters of the Froedtert Malt Company, designed by Gustav Bohland in 1948.

The twelve-foot bronze statues of Goethe and Schiller resting on a granite base. *Urban Anthropology collection.*

But arguably, the most acclaimed public art piece produced by an early German sculptor ended up in Washington Park in Milwaukee's Washington Park neighborhood.[67] The Goethe-Schiller monument, designed by Ernst Friedrich August Rietschel in 1908, depicts playwright Johann Wolfgang von Goethe and poet Friedrich von Schiller. Starting in 1902, thirty different German American cultural societies and various individuals collaborated to raise funds and donate the monument.

22.

POLITICS

*G*erman informants in Urban Anthropology's Milwaukee ethnic study described German political proclivities.

Some of them have Socialist leanings, and some of them are rabid right-wing Republicans. Many say they are pragmatic in their political leanings, and I suppose that is partly true. My mother was a Socialist; my dad a Republican.

First is [sic] *labor laws. And labor protection came from the German community in Milwaukee. The eight-hour workday came from the German community. The interest in efficient government came from the German community in Milwaukee. The opposition to vice and exploitation of women came from the German community in Milwaukee. And that used to be very severe in Milwaukee in the 1890s and 1900s.*

Without question, the Milwaukee Germans' central contribution to the city's political landscape was the "Sewer Socialist" movement. In a book published in 1982, author Elmer Beck used the term "sewer Socialists" to capture the essence of the Milwaukee experience. This term was applied to the Socialists' success in cleaning up Milwaukee both physically and politically, but the term actually had its roots in criticism from Marxist-oriented Socialists, who said that the Milwaukee party was more concerned with the pragmatics of efficient government (such as good sewers) than ideology.

MILWAUKEE'S SOCIALISTS: A BIT MORE THAN SEWERS

Milwaukee is a unique city in America. Not only was it the only large U.S. urban center to be developed by Germans—it also was the only large American city where socialism took hold. The socialist movement began in Milwaukee in the 1850s and increased in momentum until it reached its peak among workers in the early twentieth century. During that century, Socialists occupied scores of political offices in Milwaukee. These included Milwaukee's first socialist mayor Emil Seidel, who was elected in 1910. The same year that Seidel took office, Milwaukeean Victor Berger became the first Socialist sent to the U.S. Congress. Six years later, Socialist Daniel Hoan became Milwaukee's mayor and held that office for twenty-four years. Less than a decade after the Hoan era ended, Milwaukeeans elected Socialist Frank Zeidler as mayor. He held the office for twelve years, beginning in 1948. The only non-German among the major socialist office-holders was Hoan.

Both the philosophy and practices of the Milwaukee Socialists had German roots. Advocating for evolutionary rather than revolutionary

The Garden Homes neighborhood in the 1920s, a footprint of the Socialist era in Milwaukee. Save for some wear and tear, the neighborhood looks much the same today. *Milwaukee Public Library, Remember When Collection, RW2009.*

change, the formal party structure was modeled after the German socialist movement, which included the organization of subunits to the existence of a daily socialist newspaper.

The Socialist Party in Milwaukee was also grounded in German leisure-time activities. Party activists advanced socialist policies through music, plays, outdoor recreation, art, architecture, gymnastics, youth clubs and Sunday frolicking at beer gardens. They were the only political party to locally oppose national prohibition, an issue that clearly united Germans all over America. The Socialists also had a vested interest in the stability of the Milwaukee Breweries and even sold bonds to the brewery unions to support their daily newspaper.

While footprints of the years of German socialist domination in Milwaukee can be found in many areas of the city (yes, including the sewer system), the most salient neighborhood footprint is an actual neighborhood itself—Garden Homes.[68] The original fan-shaped Garden Homes Housing Project was built in the early 1920s under Mayor Daniel Hoan. It had been championed by former socialist mayor, Emil Seidel, who went on to purchase a home in the subdivision. Most of the early residents were German. The neighborhood was organized along cooperative principles, in which every resident owned shares in the neighborhood. The homes were built and sold at cost to avoid making profits. Garden Homes was the first municipally sponsored cooperative housing project in America—an unprecedented experiment.

PART 6

German Footprints on the Physical Terrain in Milwaukee Neighborhoods

23.

ARCHITECTURE

When informants in Urban Anthropology's twelve-year study of Milwaukee ethnic groups were asked to name the main contributions Germans made to Milwaukee, the topic of architecture was high on their lists.

> *I love the buildings. I love city hall. I love all the brick and woodwork and stonework on all the old buildings and the attention to detail* [that] *the Germans used back then.*

> *One of the first was house building. The most solid houses are in Milwaukee. Many of the buildings you see now have been built by German working men and German architects.*

> *Even when you go to the less wealthy parts of town and look at fairly plain—not large—buildings, you see at the tops* [of] *the buildings how the brickwork was done in certain ways. And they had different cornices. And they had medallions—those carved stone medallions above the doorways.*

One of the most interesting things about the buildings that were designed and built by Milwaukee's early Germans is that a very large proportion of them still grace Milwaukee neighborhoods today.

Institutional Buildings: Not Just Downtown

Many of Milwaukee's most stunning buildings that represent the city's cultural, civic and religious history were designed by local German American architects. Fashioned in eclectic styles with a strong representation of Flemish and German Renaissance exemplars, most of these buildings still stand today and function as they did when they were erected. These buildings include the works of immigrant Henry C. Koch, born 1841 in the Kingdom of Hanover; Alfred C. Clas, born in Wisconsin in 1860, the son of German immigrants; and immigrant Erhard Brielmaier, born in Württemberg in 1841. Koch was renowned for designing Milwaukee City Hall, the seat of city government; and Turner Hall, the home of the iconic Milwaukee Turners. Clas, together with Massachusetts native George B. Ferry, is mostly known for designing the Milwaukee Public Library, Milwaukee Auditorium and the Tower of St. John's Cathedral.

While a majority of the buildings that represent Milwaukee institutions are located in the downtown area, some are in neighborhoods that were then

The Basilica of St. Josaphat on Lincoln Avenue, circa 1910. *Basilica of St. Josaphat Foundation.*

at the city's periphery. The best example of this is the Basilica of St. Josaphat, which was designed by Erhard Brielmaier at the turn of the twentieth century. His organization, Erhard Brielmaier & Sons Co. Architects, constructed over one thousand Catholic churches, hospitals and schools throughout North America. The company assumed the work of designing the basilica for a Polish parish on Milwaukee's south side in today's Lincoln Village neighborhood.[69] The building, following the model of St. Peter's Basilica in Rome, was fashioned with a cross-shaped floorplan and a large central dome. Many of the supplies for the basilica came from salvaged materials of the Chicago Post Office and Custom House when it was razed. These were loaded up on five hundred railroad flatcars and transported to Milwaukee. The Catholic Poles of the neighborhood contributed to the building of the basilica—both in terms of their physical labor and by mortgaging their own homes to help finance the project. Brielmaier himself sometimes paid his professional laborers out of his own pockets to keep parish costs down.

Today, the Basilica of St. Josaphat remains as the beacon of the Lincoln Village neighborhood and of Milwaukee's south side in general. It is the second-most visited site in the city, just behind the Milwaukee Art Museum.

COMMERCIAL BUILDINGS: ART IN THE MINUTIAE

Commercial buildings designed by the early German architects of Milwaukee tended to have elaborate details. Even taverns had interiors of gilt, mirrors and intricate woodcarvings. Some of the most notable commercial buildings were designed by the previously mentioned Henry C. Koch, Alfred C. Clas and George B. Ferry. Others included Eugene R. Liebert, born in Berlin in 1866; Alexander C. Eschweiler, born in Boston in 1865, the son of a German immigrant; Herman Paul Schnetzky, born in Brandenburg in 1849; Charles G. Hoffmann, born in Berlin in 1832; and German immigrant Otto Strack, who arrived in Milwaukee in 1888. Koch designed the world-famous Pfister Hotel on Wisconsin Avenue in the early 1890s. Clas and Ferry were associated with a large number of downtown commercial buildings—the most famous of these being the Plankinton House Hotel (razed in 1915) and the Northwestern National Insurance Building (still standing). Liebert and Schnetzky designed the Germania building that housed the publishing empire of George Brumder (and is an apartment and office complex today). Together, with his sons, Alexander C. Eschweiler designed the Wisconsin Gas Building (still standing). Charles

An elaborate parapet on a building at Martin Luther King Drive and Brown Street. *Urban Anthropology Collection.*

G. Hoffmann was the main architect for the Pabst Brewery complex (today's the Brewery—a compound of apartments, student housing, hotels and breweries). And Otto Strack designed the opulent Pabst Theater on Wells (still standing).

While Milwaukee's most-noted architects were usually associated with Milwaukee's downtown buildings, other architects and builders left their marks along the neighborhood commercial corridors. The German trademarks included the ornate cornices, medallions above the doorways and decorative parapets. The parapets (extensions of the wall at the edge of a roof) can be curved, angular or stepped and are found frequently in the former German shopping hubs, such as Upper Third Street (today's Martin Luther King Jr. Drive), which is bordered by the Halyard Park and Brewer's Hill neighborhoods.[70] Buildings adorned with ornate parapets can even be seen on commercial streets in Riverwest and Lincoln Village—neighborhoods that were settled by Poles from the German sector of Poland who carried over the architectural tradition from their homeland.

RESIDENTIAL: ART IN THE NICETIES

As with the institutional and commercial buildings, homes designed by German architects showed great attention to detail. Styles were often eclectic, but the Germans added special effects, such as elaborately appointed gables and decorative entrance porches. One of the most beautiful homes was designed by the aforementioned Otto Strack. The mansion that once belonged to corporate officer Joseph Kalvelage was built in the Avenues West neighborhood on Kilbourn Avenue.[71] Still standing today as the Kalvelage Schloss, the home features a slated-convex mansard roof and extensive baroque detail.

Other early German architects of note who worked mainly in the residential sector included Gustave A. Dick, born in 1872 in Wisconsin, the son of German immigrants; Fred Graf, born in 1860 in Wisconsin, the son of German immigrants; Henry Messmer, born in 1871 in Wisconsin, the son of a German immigrant mother; John Menge Jr., born in 1867 in Germany; Otto C. Uehling, born in 1866 in Wisconsin, the son of German immigrants; Herman W. Buemming, born in 1876 in Ohio, the son of German immigrants; Charles F. Ringer, born in 1852 in Baden; Charles Tharinger, born in 1875 in Wisconsin, the son of German immigrants; Charles Holst,

The Kalvelage Schloss mansion, circa the 1970s. *Alan Maganye-Roshak collection.*

The Machek House, date unknown. *Urban Anthropology collection.*

born in 1877, the son of a German immigrant father; and Julius Leiser, born in Wisconsin in 1876, the son of German immigrants. Examples of their work can be found in all areas of Milwaukee but most particularly on McKinley Boulevard in the Cold Spring Park neighborhood—the same spot that had once comprised the Cold Spring Racing Course (see part 5).[72] Most of these homes still stand today. Because their owners were wealthy and also of German descent, the architectural designs tended to have an Old-World look. Common features included the end gable designed with half-timbering and stucco, reminiscent of the German Medieval half-timbering houses.

But not all remarkable homes in the Teutonic mode were built by German architects. An interesting example is the Machek House on North Nineteenth Street in the King Park neighborhood.[73] It was designed by a cabinetmaker, woodcarver and carpenter. Born in Austria or Germany (U.S. Census records vary) in 1852, Robert Machek had received a silver medal for his work on the Royal Palace in Belgrade by the king of Serbia while he was still in Europe. According to naturalization records, he arrived in the United States in 1887 and may have begun work on the Machek House soon afterwards. The house, still standing today, follows the model of medieval European cottages, with the intricacy and fine craftsmanship of its ornamentation.

24.

LANDSCAPE

German informants in Urban Anthropology's Milwaukee ethnic study frequently mentioned "good government" when discussing German contributions to the city. And this phrase was often associated with how the German leaders took care of the urban landscape.

Good government is what you see—the care of the parks and boulevards and streets.

It's just the continuing effects of the good government that the Germans brought us back then. The parks, the protected lakefront, the arts and the museums and the generally good quality of the services. Everyone in Milwaukee complains about how bad the government is, and granted, they [sic] are not as good as they used to be, but then, visitors come, and they look around, and they say this place is so well maintained. "Look, there are flowers everywhere, and they are not dug up," and you can see—like, even today, I was driving in an African American part of town, and I was really impressed. There was this boulevard. You could see lots of trees and flowers. New trees. And I thought, with all the problems this city has with money, this place still has the kind of government that puts in trees, and this is not just in downtown, where the tourists come. This was a poorish neighborhood…and I was even in San Francisco, and the streets aren't as well maintained, and you don't see the flowers everywhere and parkland—so much parkland.

A common moniker for Milwaukee is "the city of parks." The surrounding Milwaukee County boasts over 140 public parks and parkways. Much of this began in 1889, when the Milwaukee Board of Park Commissioners was first assembled. The board's purpose was to locate the best city sites to set aside for parks. This was made possible earlier that year, when the state legislature passed a series of laws that enabled the city to purchase land using money raised from the sale of bonds. The board's president, later called the "father of Milwaukee parks," was Christian Wahl. Wahl, born in Bavaria in 1829, arrived in Wisconsin in 1848; there, his family soon began to farm. After moving to Chicago and running a lucrative glue business with his brother, Christian Wahl returned to the Milwaukee area and began using his wealth to host literary and musical events, quickly advancing to the center of German-Milwaukee society. When he assumed the leadership of the Board of Park Commissioners, he put in motion the plans for the development of the city's—and later the county's—park system.

In 1936, the park planning process was taken over by Milwaukee County in order to develop parks in the city's surrounding areas. The county was immediately able to use funds and labor from several New Deal Programs (the Civil Works Administration, the Works Progress Administration and the Civilian Conservation Corps) to expand the park areas, improve infrastructure and construct many miles of trails and walks within the parks. That development has continued into the twenty-first century.

The name of Christian Wahl, the man who spawned the landscape process, appears in many formats in today's Milwaukee. A bronze bust of Wahl, designed by noted Italian artist Gaetano Trentanove, sits atop a red granite pedestal in a city park named Wahl. The Milwaukee neighborhood where the park resides is named Wahl Park.[74]

A few of the city landscapes where the Milwaukee German footprints are most striking are discussed in the following sections.

MITCHELL PARK DOMES: A BORN-AGAIN MANIFESTATION

The Mitchell Park Horticultural Conservatory had two reincarnations. The first involved Christian Wahl, and both projects were designed by German architects.

In 1839, Alexander Mitchell, a Scot, left his homeland for Milwaukee and lived to become the richest man in Wisconsin. At the turn of the twentieth century, he developed a thirty-acre private park on Milwaukee's south side called Mitchell's Grove that overlooked the Menomonee Valley (today's Mitchell Park neighborhood).[75] There, he commissioned architect and German immigrant Henry C. Koch to design an almost completely glass conservatory that was inspired by the Crystal Palace in London, England—the centerpiece of Britain's Great Exhibition. Completed in 1898, Mitchell used the conservatory to showcase plant and flower collections to his guests.

On Mitchell's death, the first reincarnation of Mitchell's Grove took place. A massive 24.5-acre tract of the grove (including the conservatory) was purchased by the newly formed Board of Park Commissioners, headed by Christian Wahl. The conservatory, then called the Mitchell Park Horticultural Conservatory, became a major destination for Milwaukeeans of all walks of life. The Easter flower show drew crowds from all across Wisconsin and beyond.

However, by 1955, the conservatory had aged and became a hazard to visitors. County officials feared a good wind might topple it. A second reincarnation was about to take place. County officials and concerned

The original Mitchell Park Horticultural Conservatory, shown here in 1910. Another German immigrant, Cyril Colnik, was an ironworks artist and created the gates at the entry. They are still on display at today's Floral Show Dome. *Milwaukee School of Engineering Archives.*

citizens held a design competition that attracted thirty-three architects from all around the world. The competition was won by a local Milwaukeean, Donald L. Grieb, the grandson of a German immigrant. Three beehive-shaped glass domes were erected, all connected to a lobby area. Then known as the Mitchell Park Domes, the conservatory featured a Floral Show Dome, a Tropical Dome and a Desert Dome. The project was dedicated in 1965 by First Lady Lady Bird Johnson.

While today, some county officials argue that the aging process for the domes might soon necessitate a third reincarnation, about 250,000 visitors from over one hundred counties still arrive annually to view the stunning floral displays.

UIHLEIN FIELD: FROM POLO TO SOCCER

In 1947, Robert and Lorraine "Lorry" (née Glaeser) Uihlein purchased a parcel of land at Seventy-First Street and Good Hope Road that would become Milwaukee Polo Field and, later, Uihlein Field. The land, at the time, was in Granville Township, which has since been annexed by Milwaukee, placing Uihlein Field in the city's Menomonee River Hills East neighborhood.[76] Robert Uihlein was the grandson of German immigrant August Uihlein, who, together with his brother Henry, had assumed ownership of the Joseph Schlitz Brewing Company on the death of Joseph Schlitz. Robert had a great love of horses, and he and Lorry purchased the land for polo games. They developed the land themselves, dynamiting away forested areas and tilling and grading the land. Lorry even drove the tractor. For over forty years, Milwaukeeans enjoyed Sunday afternoon polo games at Uihlein Field.

Robert Uihlein died of leukemia in 1976, after spending his last five years running the Joseph Schlitz Brewing Company. Lorry and her children took over the management of the polo field. In the meantime, another sport was gaining popularity in the city—soccer. The Milwaukee Kickers Soccer Club had been formally organized in 1968, with 78 members, and it grew exponentially in the late twentieth century—by 2020, it had a membership of 8,500. In the 1980s, the club sought a permanent venue for its games. The polo field was chosen. Lorry Uihlein worked with the Kickers, pledging over $2 million to the project, and she agreed to the sale and transfer of the property. However, property tax and environmental issues arose, and the sale appeared doomed. The Kickers Board of Trustees and club officers worked with Milwaukee County supervisors and Milwaukee County executive Thomas Ament to have the county purchase the land. Forming a partnership, the club and county resolved the complications and agreed to issue a twenty-year bond to buy the land and build an indoor soccer field, with the club paying back the bond issue. The indoor field was erected through a working relationship with Uihlein Architects and Milwaukee County administration. Today, Uihlein Field is a Milwaukee County park known as Uihlein Soccer Park.

HENRY MAIER FESTIVAL PARK: THE HOME OF SUMMERFEST AND MUCH MORE

Summerfest was the vision of Milwaukee mayor Henry Maier. The grandson of German immigrants, Maier was born Henry Walter David Nelke in 1918. His father died when Henry was young, and he later adopted the Maier surname of his stepfather. Serving longer than any other Milwaukee mayor, Maier made the planning and implementation of Summerfest his top priority during the mid- to late 1960s.

Today, Milwaukee's Summerfest is promoted as the "World's Largest Music Festival"—a claim supported by an annual attendance of 800,000 to 900,000 participants and certification of the title by Guinness World Records in 1999. The event runs in early summer on Milwaukee's lakefront. However, the first Summerfest was not on the lakefront and could hardly be called a music festival. Spread over a multitude of city venues, the original gig included events such as a water ski show, a stock car race, a boat parade, magicians, circus acts, a *Jack & the Beanstalk* puppet show, a boat race, museum exhibits, a Greek Orthodox picnic and performances by Wisconsin Idea Theater and the National Ballet of Mexico. While the first Summerfest had some success, the second year was devastating. Horrific weather forced the cancellation of the event's last day, and the financial losses returned the event to the planning table.

Maier and his Summerfest panel of business and civic leaders sought a central location for the festival. They selected an abandoned strip of land on the lakefront in the Historic Third Ward neighborhood that had once been an airport and served as a Nike missile site during the Cold War.[77] To prevent cancellations of events due to weather, in 1970, stages were constructed of wooden slabs atop concrete blocks. The plan worked, and the construction of other buildings continued throughout the 1970s

The Summerfest grounds in 1972. *Alan Maganye-Roshak.*

and the 1980s, including that of an amphitheater with a twenty-three-thousand-seat capacity.

Informally known as the "Summerfest Grounds," the strip of land was later named Henry Maier Festival Park. Today, the park also accommodates a large number of additional events, including ethnic festivals, Laborfest, Pridefest, a pet festival and others. It represents the most significant footprint of Maier's tenure in office.

But less positive footprints also remain.

25

URBAN RENEWAL

*I*n the era of urban renewal in Milwaukee, German development wasn't what they added to the landscape, but what they removed.

When informants were asked about Milwaukee policies that affected neighborhoods or ethnic groups in Urban Anthropology's neighborhood oral histories or the ethnic study, the policies cited most often were urban renewal and freeway building in the mid-1900s that razed entire neighborhoods, many of them ethnic. The discussions were overwhelmingly critical. The bulk of urban renewal and freeway building took place under two German Milwaukee mayors, Frank Zeidler and Henry Maier. While responsibility for freeway building was transferred from the city to Milwaukee County's Expressway Commission in late 1953, the massive system of highways that displaced many Milwaukee neighborhoods was initially championed by Mayor Zeidler. Both mayors assumed the responsibility for implementing urban renewal, but they did so in different ways.

Urban renewal projects were made feasible with the passage of Title I of the Housing Act of 1949, which gave federal aid for slum clearance to eliminate blight. Local governments could then receive funds to raze slum areas and rebuild them. But in response to criticism that the federally funded projects displaced and disrupted entire communities, the U.S. government passed the Housing Act of 1954, which then gave money for conservation as well as rehabilitation projects. Hence, there were two tracts: (1) redevelopment, or demolition and site clearance with cleared properties sold to private and public companies, and (2) conservation, or improvements to areas to prevent blight and halt decline of middle-aged areas.

Beginning in 1955, Milwaukee initiated a series of urban renewal projects under Mayor Frank Zeidler. Zeidler, a grandson of German immigrants, was the city's third socialist mayor, having served from 1948 to 1960. All of the projects were designed using the redevelopment tract. Areas that were deemed slums were to be razed, and under the plan, residents could eventually access future public housing at sites that were dispersed across the city. When Zeidler declined to run for office again in 1960, Henry Maier, the grandson of German immigrants, tossed his hat in the ring and was elected mayor. Almost all of the urban renewal projects that were completed during his term in office were inherited from Zeidler. However, Maier slowed the progress of slum removal, drawing the frequently reported public wrath of Frank Zeidler. In a *Milwaukee Sentinel* article that was printed on October 4, 1962, Zeidler accused Maier of placing more emphasis on conservation and rehabilitation than on complete demolition. Frank Zeidler was quoted in the article as saying, "There is no substitute for slum clearance," arguing for complete blight removal and replanning of the areas under urban renewal. Maier claimed he preferred aid to property owners to rehabilitate their homes.

Even though the razing of older areas gradually slowed under Maier, Milwaukee lost part or all of many of its older but closely knit neighborhoods. Among the ethnic neighborhoods that were completely razed were Little Italy, African American Bronzeville and Little Puerto Rico. Among the ethnic neighborhoods that were partially razed were Irish Merrill Park and Polish Lincoln Village/Baran Park. Two of the larger removal projects are highlighted in the following sections.

LOWER THIRD WARD: LITTLE ITALY AND THE "LITTLE PINK CHURCH"

The Lower Third Ward project was the first urban renewal program initiated under Mayor Frank Zeidler. The Third Ward region that was slated for demolition, located in today's Historic Third Ward neighborhood, was home to first-, second- and third-generation Italians from Sicily.[78] They had moved into an area that had been vacated by the Irish following the great Third Ward fire of 1892. The Italians built a strong ethnic community in the ward. By 1920, the neighborhood had forty-five grocers; two spaghetti

The Little Pink Church on Van Buren, circa 1957. *Italian Community Center.*

factories; a Festa Italiana; and Commission Row, where fruit and vegetable wholesalers hawked their wares at the curbsides of grocers and restaurants, drawing customers from every part of the city. Most importantly, the Italians had built the Blessed Virgin of Pompeii on Jackson Street. Called the "Little Pink Church" because of its pink-painted bricks, the house of worship was the spiritual center of the Third Ward Italians.

By the 1950s, most of the buildings in the ward were past their prime. Many had been built prior to 1900. The Zeidler administration made the decision to make the ward the city's first redevelopment project. When news of property demolition was passed on to the community, the response was fierce. Willard Downing, the executive director of the Milwaukee Redevelopment Authority, one of the agencies responsible for implementing the project, later described the reaction in a 1960 article in the *Milwaukee Journal.* He discussed how residents, business owners and spiritual leaders fought the condemnation. Two public hearings were held: the first lasted from 7:00 p.m. until midnight; the second lasted from 7:00 p.m. to 2:00 a.m. Property owners and cultural leaders argued that the neighborhood was not a slum and that the demolition would destroy their community. Battles continued from 1954 until May 1957, when the demolition began.

Ultimately, over two hundred buildings were condemned and razed, and the community was forced to find homes elsewhere, returning only on Sundays for services at the Blessed Virgin of Pompeii. The population of the Third Ward, which had been 2,402 in 1950, dropped to 258 in 1960. The construction of the I-794 Freeway completed the demolition in 1967, when the "Little Pink Church" was also bulldozed.

While the Italian community still mourns the dispersal of this community today, people across the city concurred. The following quotes are from informants in Urban Anthropology's Milwaukee ethnic study and neighborhood oral histories. In them, they discussed this loss.

> *It made no sense. Most of the homes needed just a little work. They could have spent their money there and not broken up the community. But urban renewal took out everything. The culture, the community.*

> *No policy that I can think of had much effect in my neighborhood, but I'd say there was* [a policy effect] *in the Third Ward. We came there to see the Italian processions and the festivals. No one could believe it when the city said they were going to condemn this neighborhood.*

> *And they knocked down the Pompeii Church.....Nothing really impacted us as much as that, except for when the city came in and condemned all of the houses. They condemned all of our houses, and we had to move out. We had an all-brick home, and we had to move out of it because it was condemned because the city said it was, and there was nothing we could do about it.*

> *It was the first urban renewal project the city undertook, and they were well intentioned, but they didn't realize the devastation it brought to the community....I know, in Boston, they wouldn't let them do it, and they are so happy they didn't do it. The* [Italian] *north end is a real significant part of Boston* [today].

Footprints of the once-thriving Italian community remain in the neighborhood, which is now called the Historic Third Ward. A historic marker of the Blessed Virgin of Pompeii was erected in 1977 by Pompeii Men's Club and the City of Milwaukee at the church's original location, now at the intersection of the Van Buren Street Exit 1E Ramp of I-794 and Jackson Street. Milwaukeeans have also made moves to bring "Little Italy" back to the Third Ward. When the Italians of southeastern Wisconsin decided to build a community center, they built the sixty-thousand-square-foot Italian Community Center back in their old neighborhood on East Chicago Street. When Commission Row finally closed, an indoor, upscale version of the former market was erected in 2005 on North Water at the northern boundary of the Historic Third Ward, which is called the Milwaukee Public Market.

BRONZEVILLE: THE RAZING OF EIGHT THOUSAND HOMES AND THE COMMERCIAL DISTRICT

The losses experienced by the Italians of the Third Ward were moderate compared to the losses experienced by the African Americans of Bronzeville. The combination of clearances from urban renewal and freeway building cost this community over eight thousand homes and nearly its entire business district.

The once-thriving community of Bronzeville that was centered on Walnut Street was built up during the Great Migration. The area included today's neighborhoods of Halyard Park, Hillside, Haymarket and a section of Triangle North.[79] When African Americans began arriving in large numbers to Milwaukee between 1930 and 1960, a combination of factors worked to turn an already aging area into a slum. These factors included redlining in the private housing market, laws in which municipalities zoned industrial areas that surrounded Black neighborhoods to keep Black people contained in those areas, restrictive agreements in which deeds stipulated who could and could not purchase the property and the refusal of financial institutions to approve mortgage loans for African Americans. Almost none of the buildings were owned by Black people themselves.

The appearance of the Bronzeville area had seriously declined by 1950, but the community itself was vibrant. African American Bronzeville managed its own churches, grocers, drugstores, recreational centers, hotels, movie theaters, newspapers, funeral homes, nightclubs, record stores, restaurants and social clubs of ten to fifteen members each that sponsored their own weekend entertainment and donated to worthy local causes. By 1959, there were 160 religious, fraternal and social organizations in the area, and most of them were social clubs. The Bronzeville nightclubs featured name

Walnut Street in the 1950s (see the Regal Theater in the background). *Wisconsin Black Historical Society.*

entertainers, such as Duke Ellington, Billie Holiday and Louis Armstrong, and they attracted thousands of White as well as Black patrons. The slogan of a popular restaurant, Larry's Chicken Shack on Walnut, reflected the spirit of the area: "If you live and play in Bronzeville, it is a joy and pride, and Larry's luncheonette is the best in southern fried."

Two urban renewal ventures—the Hillside Neighborhood Redevelopment Project and Haymarket Square Redevelopment Project—began during Frank Zeidler's term and continued during Henry Maier's. With the promise of public housing to come, the community did not initially react to the first signs of slum removal in the late 1950s. But when the urban renewal efforts and construction of two major freeway corridors removed nearly all of the community's commercial district on Walnut Street and threatened to take out more blocks, residents united in opposition. Under the leadership of James Richardson, residents formed an improvement group in 1960 to remove signs of blight at the western edge of the razed area in hopes of blockading further demolition efforts. They organized cleanups, built and attached flower boxes to homes and pressured absentee landlords to rehab their buildings by sending photographs of the landlords' own homes and those they had turned into rental properties in Bronzeville to newspapers.

By 1965, the informal improvement group had grown into a formal organization, the Walnut Improvement Council (WAICO). The organization moved with a vengeance, promising to empower residents to wrench them out of the hands of city planners. WAICO recruited architects to help rebuild the community, attracted celebrities to champion the cause and raised $515,000 for paint and supplies to improve the area. By 1969, all threats of further bulldozing disappeared.

But residents who had lost their homes and most of their once-cohesive community never forgot. The Walnut Street Social Club Reunion was formed and, at the time of this writing, still meets every year in Carver Park to recall days in old Bronzeville. Urban Anthropology Inc. conducted interviews with a sample of the former residents.

The loss of Bronzeville was the breakdown of the village. The Whites had people moving them into the projects and those [African Americans] *with a little money moved to the suburbs. It was then the image of who we were that came from the Whites. Before that, it had been a localized culture. Before that, you took care of your own—you watched other people's kids, made sure your neighborhood was nice and safe. After the move, we lost that.*

Oh, they didn't know too much about what was going to happen, and then they found out. And what that did was—they removed eight thousand homes. They wanted to just get rid of them. And they didn't care about the people who lived there, just wanted to make it look better, you know. That didn't change the conditions, you know....It was callous.

> *It took so long before people started saying, "Say, what happened there? Why did they do that* [razing Bronzeville]*?" But I say, "You watch out because it can happen again. All you need is someone that just likes his power."*

Today, a coalition of African American activists, in partnership with the City of Milwaukee, are attempting to rebuild Bronzeville. The vision is the creation of a new commercial and entertainment district that will mirror the area's past. At the time of this writing, a large number of installments are already in place.

PART 7

Efforts to Remove German Footprints from Milwaukee Neighborhoods

26

WORLD WAR I

*T*he energy that Milwaukee Germans expended in promenading their culture was ultimately sapped when Germany became America's enemy in the years after the nation's entrance into the two world wars. During World War I, sauerkraut was renamed "liberty cabbage," the Pabst Theater halted production of German plays for the entire 1918 season, student enrolment in Milwaukee German classes dropped from thirty thousand in 1916 to just four hundred by 1918, Schmidts became Smiths, Schneiders became Taylors, Germans were fined or jailed for remarks about Liberty bonds, the literary works of Schiller and Goethe disappeared from city classrooms and the Wisconsin Loyalty Legion initiated a boycott of the German press. This latter action resulted in the removal of a salient German footprint in the city.

GERMANIA STATUE: "GONE GIRL"

The German press was ubiquitous during the German Athens generations in Milwaukee. By the 1880s, German-language newspapers had more readers in the city than English dailies. The Germania building, with its towers resembling spiked Prussian helmets, was home to the largest German publishing house in the United States. Standing today as a luxury apartment complex, the building is located on West Wells Street in the Westown neighborhood.[80] However, it is missing one feature—a ten-foot-tall, bronze statue called *Germania*—a goddess representation

The Germania building with a bronze statue of Germania above the entrance, circa pre-1918. *Milwaukee County Historical Society.*

that personified the German nation and Germans as a whole. But during World War I, when the outcries against displays of German culture were at their strongest, the building's owners feared vandalism and commissioned a noted metalsmith, Cyril Colnik, and his crew of workers, to take down the statue in the dead of the night. Colnik and his crew also chiseled off the building's nameplate. Henceforth, for decades, the structure became known as the Brumder building.

What happened to the Germania statue is a Milwaukee mystery. Colnik originally hid the lady in his Ornamental Iron Shop. Save for being loaned out for a convention at the old Milwaukee Auditorium about 1940, nothing remains of the bronze goddess but rumored sightings.

Deutscher Club: A Most Exclusive Clubhouse

Standing at 900 Wisconsin Avenue on the border of Milwaukee's Westown and Marquette neighborhoods is the very elegant Wisconsin Club.[81] Over the years, the French Second Empire mansion has hosted dignitaries, such as President Ulysses S. Grant, President Theodore Roosevelt, prominent abolitionist Julia Ward Howe, the Grand Duke Alexis of Russia, Prussia's Prince Henry and President Grover Cleveland. Membership in this club is steep, a dress code is still enforced and the menus have no prices. But its name was not always the Wisconsin Club.

The mansion was originally the home of Wisconsin's wealthiest citizen, Scottish-born Alexander Mitchell. Built in 1848, Mitchell updated and expanded his Mitchell House many times. Eight years after Mitchell's death, his family sold the home to the German American Deutscher Club. Established in 1891 to provide fellowship for Milwaukee's affluent German businessmen, the Deutscher Club first made its home in the Nunnemacher Grand Opera House building on East Wells. When this building burned down in 1895, the club sought a new clubhouse. Initially leasing the Mitchell House, the Deutscher Club made the decision to purchase it in 1898 for $165,000.

Between 1898 and 1917, the Deutscher Club maintained the mansion as a private meeting place for German businessmen, adding a dining hall and bowling alleys in 1906. The rooms on the upper floor were considerably remodeled. However, when America declared war on Germany in 1917, the club decided to downplay its Germanness and adopted the new name of the Wisconsin Club. Under the new moniker, the organization continued as an exclusive private club. While today, very little about the Wisconsin Club appears German, it continues to attract members and boasts being in the top 5 percent of U.S. private clubs in sales of food and beverages.

German-English Academy: A Case of Name Dropping

Founded by wealthy German immigrants, the German-English Academy opened in 1851. Unhappy with the city's public schools, the founders—many Forty-Eighters and Turners—wanted instruction in German as well as English. They also sought to incorporate German educational components, such as kindergarten, physical education, drawing, singing and domestic science, into

The original German-English Academy building at 1020 North Broadway, circa 1930. Today, it is owned by the Milwaukee School of Engineering. *Milwaukee School of Engineering Archives.*

the classroom. During its first year, the school had forty students who paid fifty cents a month for tuition. Classes met in the home of its first teacher, Peter Engelmann.

From that time on, the student body grew exponentially. In 1891 and 1892, a new building was erected for the school. The structure had two sections: one was financed by the Pfister-Vogel family and the other by the Milwaukee Turner Society. With ample space, the academy then included a natural science museum, physics and chemistry labs, domestic science classes for girls and a manual arts program for boys. Over the years, the academy graduated many teachers for Milwaukee's public school system.

However, during World War I, the German-English Academy confronted the distrust of all things German and renamed the institution the Milwaukee University School. The school later moved to the Milwaukee suburb of River Hills in 1927.

The academy's first building still stands in Milwaukee's East Town neighborhood and is listed in the National Register of Historic Places.[82]

27.

WORLD WAR II

*D*uring Urban Anthropology's twelve-year ethnic study, some German informants were advanced enough in age to recall the social and political pressures their families faced during World War II.

Politics are rough for Germans. During the war years, we started playing cards because we would get into arguments about politics. Turners was a German organization. The police would walk in and try and get info on who took a stand for Hitler. License numbers were written down.

Not only did we fight the German backlash, we fought the Germans themselves....It was the Nazis. It wasn't the Germans. There's a distinction. There are the German folks, and then there's the Nazis. A German is not a Nazi and a Nazi is not a German.

My mother was so proud to be German. There was this time in the nineteenth and maybe turn of the twentieth century when German everything—philosophy, music, science—ruled the world. There was this sense of maybe superiority. But then came the wars, and the Germans here are just supposed to be Americans and forget all that. You couldn't say anything good about Germany or Germans. It was too humiliating.

And for some Milwaukee Germans, the wrong words around the wrong people could have led to imprisonment.

THE HOUSE OF CORRECTION: GERMAN INTERNMENT

Over the years, much attention has been paid to the internment of the Japanese during World War II, but little has been reported about the internment of Italians and Germans. In fact, one of these internment camps was right in the middle of today's Milwaukee neighborhood of Havenwoods, and it was mainly organized for the detention of local Germans.[83]

In the early twentieth century, Milwaukee County began purchasing farmland near North Hopkins in what was then Granville Township (later to be annexed to the city of Milwaukee). The 402-acre site was set aside for the construction of a replacement prison for the House of Refuge that had operated on West Windlake Avenue but had outgrown its space. Surrounded by farms and forest, the new prison opened in 1917 and was named the House of Correction. Prisoners became farmers, bakers and artisans, tending crops, milking over seventy nearby Holsteins and crafting furniture for the prison's Granville Chair Factory.

In 1941, just days after the attack on Pearl Harbor, the U.S. government began using the House of Correction to intern Milwaukee Germans. German aliens who had been accused of being Nazi sympathizers were rounded up by local authorities and faced a federal review board that determined who would be interned and who would be paroled. At one point, sixty-one German men, one Italian man and seven German women were held at the facility. One of the German men was the gardener of Wisconsin's then-governor Julius Peter Heil.

Most of those who were interned remained at the facility for the duration of World War II. At the close of the conflict, the United States Army seized the House of Correction and used it as a disciplinary barracks for soldiers and prisoners of war. While the House of Correction still exists today at another location in the Milwaukee suburb of Franklin, the site of the original complex was officially declared the Havenwoods State Forest in 1979.

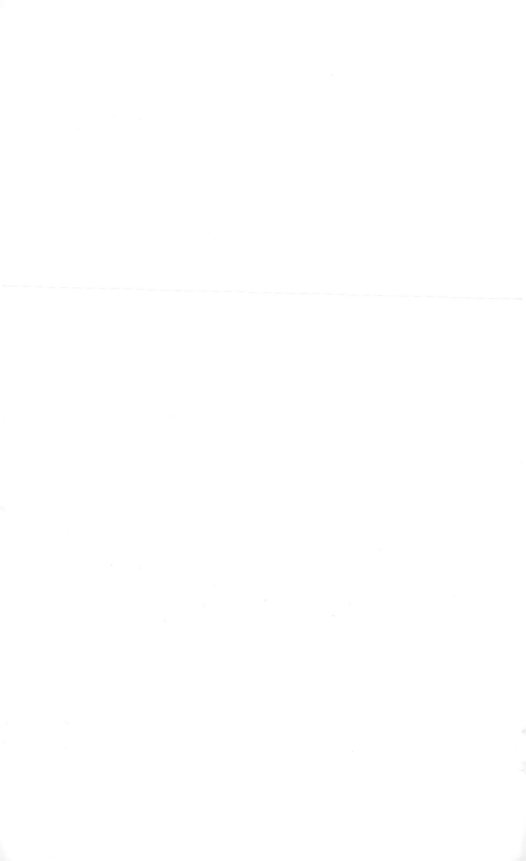

PART 8

*Restoring Milwaukee's
German Essence*

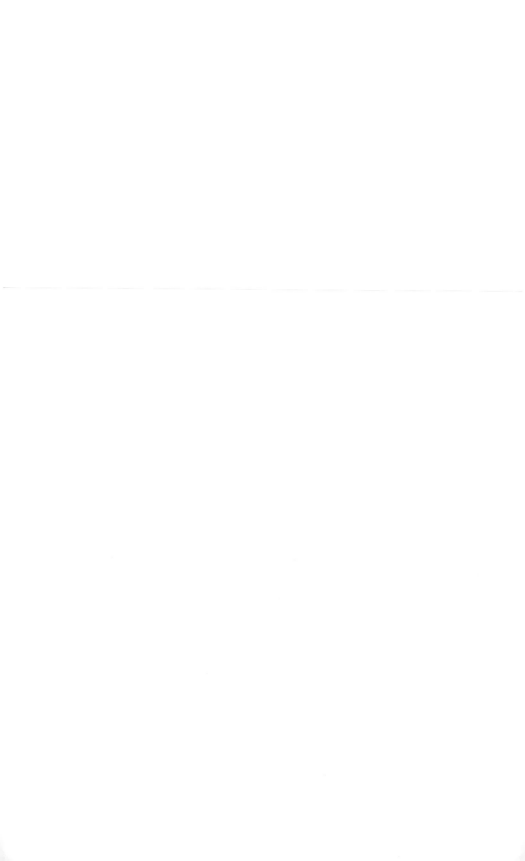

28

SUMMARIZING THE FOOTPRINTS

At the time of this writing, over 1,200 Milwaukee informants have been interviewed during Urban Anthropology's studies of the city's ethnic groups and neighborhoods. Because of the profound impact that Germans had on the city and its neighborhoods, it was inevitable that informants would perceive both positive and negative legacies.

THE POSITIVES: "YOU THINK 'SOLID'"

The overwhelming number of remarks on German footprints in Milwaukee was positive. These included omnipresent phrases, such as "solidly built homes," "best breweries," "most parks" and "German Athens," in reference to the high culture the Germans brought (and left behind) in Milwaukee. One informant discussed the positive remains as follows:

> *When you think of what the Germans left behind, you think "solid." Things were solid. The buildings were solid. The parks, the streets, theaters. The families that ran the businesses were solid. Things were built to last.*

Much of what the Germans constructed in Milwaukee nearly a century or more ago still stands in the city's neighborhoods with relatively minor alterations. Examples include houses of worship, cemeteries and clubhouses from the first German settlements; German place names on neighborhoods and streets; commercial hubs, such as Upper Third Street (today's Martin Luther King Jr. Drive), Burleigh and Vliet; eateries, including Mader's and Von Trier; food producing enterprises, such as Ma Baensch's Herring and Usinger's Sausages; educational institutions, including Mount Mary, Alverno College and Milwaukee School of Engineering; machine shop Falk Corporation (today's Rexnord Falk); theaters, such as the Oriental, Downer, Riverside and Pabst; architectural masterpieces, including the Basilica of St. Josaphat, the Mitchell Park Domes and Milwaukee City Hall; the Goethe-Schiller monument; and the footprint of the city's socialist era cemented in the Garden Homes neighborhood.

Other German creations have been repurposed but retain some aspect of their past in the names or functions. Examples of repurposed structures that retained the original German family names include the Joseph Schlitz Brewing Company complex that later became the Schlitz Office Park, the Valentin Blatz Brewing Company complex that was transformed into the Blatz Apartments and Condos, the Trostel Tannery that became the Trostel Square Apartments and Uihlein Polo Field that was converted into Uihlein Soccer Park. Examples of repurposed structures that retained similar functions include the Pabst Brewery complex, which became, in part, the Brewhouse Inn and Suites; buildings of the original Concordia College complex that were reincarnated as the Potawatomi Wygema Campus; Schlitz Beer Garden, which became Carver Park; the Trivoli Palm Garden building that was transformed into the home of a new initiator of social life, NEWaukee; and the Lutheran/Deaconess Hospital grounds that eventually became a neighborhood-healing nonprofit, City on the Hill.

THE NEGATIVES: "DESTROYED COMMUNITIES"

When informants in Urban Anthropology's neighborhood oral histories and the ethnic study were asked about Milwaukee policies that effected neighborhoods or ethnic groups, the policies cited most often were urban renewal and freeway building in the 1950s and 1960s that razed entire neighborhoods. The bulk of urban renewal and freeway building took place under two Milwaukee German mayors, Frank Zeidler and Henry Maier. While responsibility for freeway building was transferred from the city to Milwaukee County in late 1953, the massive system of highways that displaced many Milwaukee residents was initially championed by

Mayor Zeidler. Both mayors assumed the responsibility for implementing urban renewal.

Informants' responses were overwhelmingly critical. The residents of most of the bulldozed blocks had either been people of color or members of close-knit ethnic groups. Phrases the informants used most often included "destroyed communities," "tore neighborhoods apart" and "racist."

> *They* [political leaders] *thought it would be a good place for urban renewal to just tear down the houses, get rid of the people, especially the ones with the wrong color....They got no money to help them relocate; they were simply thrown out.*

Among the ethnic neighborhoods that were completely leveled were Little Puerto Rico, African American Bronzeville and Little Italy. Among the ethnic neighborhoods that were partially leveled were Irish Merrill Park and Polish Lincoln Village/Baran Park. The African American areas of the city took the greatest hit, with the loss of over eight thousand homes and the Black commercial district on Walnut Street.

29.

WAYS MILWAUKEE IS
RESURRECTING ITS GERMANNESS

*R*egardless of the criticism of razed neighborhoods under two German Milwaukee mayors, the contributions that Germans made to Milwaukee were viewed favorably by an overwhelming number of informants in the Urban Anthropology studies. This attitude is reflected in current city developments. In recent years, there has been a movement to restore a semblance of Milwaukee's German Athens sentiment.

AT THE CITY'S CENTER:
(THE FORMER) OLD WORLD THIRD AND THE DEER DISTRICT

No area in Milwaukee better represented the spirit of German Athens than the Westown neighborhood.[84] It hosted many of the Forty-Eighters and their clubhouse, Turner Hall. It accommodated the Germania building and the largest German publisher in the nation. It was home to the Pabst Theater that was once labeled "the finest in the country."

Over the past fifty years, Milwaukee has built on these institutions and is resurrecting some of the German essence. In 1984, Milwaukee's Common Council passed a resolution to rename six blocks on North Third Street to Old World Third Street, and in 2021, it was renamed again to Dr. Martin Luther King Jr. Drive (MLK). The blocks between West Wisconsin Avenue and West McKinley Avenue represented the

Christkindlmarket in the Deer District in 2019. *Urban Anthropology collection.*

last intact portion of the original German retail district in the Westown neighborhood. Fifteen of the buildings were built between 1858 and 1910, and nearly all of the original shops had German names, including two that remain today—Usinger's Sausage and Mader's Restaurant. Many of the Italianate, Victorian Gothic and Romanesque-styled buildings were designed by noted German architects. The district was listed in the National Register of Historic Places in 1987 and in the State Register of Historic Places in 1989.

Over the years, new establishments have increased the German presence on Old World Third (now MLK). These include the Milwaukee Brat House, which serves the traditional Milwaukee-style brat, and the Old German Beer Hall, which was fashioned after Munich's world-renowned Hofbräuhaus. When the Milwaukee Bucks made the decision to build a new basketball complex one block west of Old World Third (now MLK) between 2016 and 2018, they worked with German American Events LLC to include German components. Most notable is the Christkindlmarket, which was inspired by the original *Christkindlesmarkt* in Nuremberg. Open on the Fiserv Forum Grounds (now called the Deer District) between mid-November and December 31, the market offers thirty vendors in traditional candy cane–striped huts, German food, handcrafted ethnic gifts and a broad lineup of local entertainment. It attracts approximately thirty-five thousand people each season.

IN THE NEIGHBORHOODS:
THE RETURN OF THE BEER GARDENS

But the attempts to restore the city's German essence are not limited to the Westown neighborhood and downtown. They are also happening in neighborhoods at the periphery of the city's center. Beer gardens were very much a part of the German Athens era. Created mostly by breweries, they were the public parks of their time. They were places for the entire family to enjoy an appealing communal space that also offered the chance to imbibe in Milwaukee's most prolific liquid product—beer.

In 2012, Milwaukee opened its first beer garden since Prohibition. The Milwaukee County Parks Department converted two restored fire trucks into mobile beer trucks and equipped them with twelve craft brews from the local Sprecher Brewery. The trucks travel around Milwaukee County parks during two simultaneously running tours between May and September. The excursions run for three weeks, and each are called the "Roll Out the Barrel Tour" and the "Pass Me a Pint Tour." To date, the following City of Milwaukee parks have been included in the tours: Juneau Park in the east side Yankee Hill neighborhood, Cooper Park in the northwest side Cooper Park neighborhood, Washington Park in the west side Washington Park neighborhood and Lake Park in the east side Lake Park neighborhood—the latter being the site of Milwaukee's very first beer

A Beer Garden truck with patrons in a Milwaukee park. *Urban Anthropology collection.*

garden, "Lueddemann's-on-the-Lake."[85] Park dwellers order their beers from bartenders at truck windows and join their families at picnic benches.

During this time period, the city's south side Bay View neighborhood has also created beer gardens that are open for the entire warm-weather season.[86] These include the Humboldt Park Beer Garden, which serves craft beers, hard soda, cider, wine and nonalcoholic beverages; and the South Shore Beer Garden, which serves beer, hard soda and wine and also offers farm-to-table entrées and live music one night a week. More and more, the recent beer gardens are resembling their German prototypes.

NOTES

Introduction

1. Urban Anthropology Inc. complies with human subjects' protocols of formal research. Informants sign informed consent documents that stipulate anonymity. Hence, names are not provided with the quotes.

Part 1

2. Also known as Kilbourn Town. Neighborhood boundaries: (north) West McKinley Avenue; (south) I-794 East; (east) Milwaukee River; (west) I-43.
3. Neighborhood boundaries: (north) West Walnut Street; (south) West Highland Avenue; (east) Highway 43; (west) North Twentieth Street, partial.
4. Neighborhood boundaries: (north) Milwaukee Mitchell International Airport; (south) West College Avenue; (east) South Howell Avenue; (west) South Third Street.
5. Neighborhood boundaries: (north) North Leon Terrace; (south) West Mill Road; (east) North Leon Terrace; (west) North 107th Street.
6. Neighborhood boundaries: (north) East Clybourn Street; (south) Erie Street; (east) Lake Michigan; (west) Milwaukee River.
7. Neighborhood boundaries: (north) East Kenwood Boulevard; (south) East Locust Street; (east) North Lake Drive; (west) North Oakland Avenue.
8. Neighborhood boundaries: (north) East Kenwood Boulevard; (south) East Locust Street; (east) North Lake Drive; (west) North Oakland Avenue.

9. Neighborhood boundaries: (north) East Ogden Avenue; (south) East State Street; (east) North Lincoln Memorial Drive; (west) North Jackson Street.

10. Neighborhood boundaries: (north) West McKinley Avenue; (south) I-794 East; (east) Milwaukee River; (west) I-43.

11. Jones Island neighborhood boundaries: (north) Milwaukee River, partial; (south) East Bay Street, partial; (east) Lake Michigan; (west) Kinnickinnic River.

12. Neighborhood boundaries: (north) West Silver Spring Drive; (south) West Capitol Drive; (east) North Teutonia Avenue; (west) North Sherman Boulevard.

13. Neighborhood boundaries: (north) West Walnut Street; (south) West Highland Avenue; (east) Highway 43; (west) North Twentieth Street, partial.

Part 2

14. Neighborhood boundaries: (north) Mitchell International Airport; (south) West College Avenue; (east) South Howell Avenue; (west) South Third Street.

15. Neighborhood boundaries: (north) West Wisconsin Avenue; (south) I-94; (east) North Thirty-Ninth Street; (west) Menomonee River.

16. Neighborhood boundaries: (north) West Good Hope; (south) North Fond du Lac; (east) North Ninety-Ninth Street; (west) North 107th Street.

17. Also known as Lindsay Heights. Neighborhood boundaries: (north) West Burleigh Street; (south) West North Avenue; (east) Highway 43; (west) North Nineteenth Street.

18. Neighborhood boundaries: (north) East Capitol Drive; (south) Milwaukee River; (east) Milwaukee River; (west) North Holton Street.

19. Neighborhood boundaries: (north) I-94; (south) West Main Street; (east) South Hawley Road; (west) South Seventieth Street.

20. Neighborhood boundaries: (north) West Pierce Street; (south) West Greenfield Avenue; (east) South Cesar Drive; (west) South Layton Avenue.

21. Neighborhood boundaries: (north) Kinnickinnick River; (south) East Morgan Avenue; (east) Lake Michigan; (west) I-94.

22. Neighborhood boundaries: (north) East Locust Street; (south) East Kane Place; (east) North Terrace Avenue, partial, North Wahl Avenue; (west) North Prospect Avenue, partial, North Downer Avenue.

23. Neighborhood boundaries: (north) West Hampton Avenue; (south) West Congress Street; (east) North Sherman Boulevard; (west) West Parkway Drive.

24. Neighborhood boundaries: (north) I-94; (south) West Dickinson Street; (east) South Seventieth Street; (west) Highway 45.

Part 3

25. Harambee neighborhood boundaries: (north) West Keefe Avenue; (south) West North Avenue; (east) North Holton Street; (west) Highway 43. Riverwest neighborhood boundaries: (north) East Capitol Drive; (south) Milwaukee River; (east) Milwaukee River; (west) North Holton Street. Brewer's Hill neighborhood boundaries: (north) West North Avenue; (south) West Walnut Street; (east) North Holton Street; (west) Dr. Martin Luther King Jr. Drive.

26. Park View neighborhood boundaries: (north) West Galena Street; (south) West Vliet Street; (east) North Seventeenth Street; (west) North Twentieth Street. King Park neighborhood boundaries: (north) West Walnut Street; (south) West Highland Avenue; (east) Highway 43; (west) North Twentieth Street, partial. Midtown neighborhood boundaries: (north) West North Avenue; (south) West Highland Avenue; (east) North Twentieth Street; (west) North Thirty-First Street. Cold Spring Park boundaries: (north) West Vliet Street; (south) West Highland Boulevard; (east) North Twenty-Seventh Street; (west) North Thirty-Fifth Street. Martin Drive boundaries: (north) West Vliet Street; (south) West Martin Drive–West Highland Boulevard; (east) North Thirty-Fifth Street; (west) Wisconsin Highway 175. Washington Park neighborhood boundaries: (north) West North Avenue; (south) West Vliet Street; (east) North Thirty-Fifth Street; (west) North Forty-Seventh Street.

27. St. Joseph neighborhood boundaries: (north) West Burleigh Street; (south) West Center Street; (east) North Forty-Third Street; (west) North Sixtieth Street. Grasslyn Manor neighborhood boundaries: (north) West Capitol Drive; (south) Roosevelt Drive; (east) North Thirtieth Street; (west) North Sixtieth Street. Roosevelt Grove neighborhood boundaries: (north) West Capitol Drive; (south) West Burleigh Street; (east) North Thirtieth Street; (west) West Fond Du Lac Avenue. Sunset Height neighborhood boundaries: (north) West Capitol Drive; (south) West Burleigh Street; (east) North Thirtieth Street; (west) West Fond Du Lac Avenue. Uptown neighborhood boundaries: (north) West Fond Du Lac Ave; (south) West Burleigh St; (east) North Sherman Blvd; (west) West Roosevelt Drive. Sherman Park neighborhood boundaries: (north) West Center Street; (south) West North Avenue; (east) North Sherman Boulevard; (west) North Sixtieth Street.

28. Neighborhood boundaries: (north) West North Avenue; (south) West Walnut Street; (east) Dr. Martin Luther King Jr. Drive; (west) North Halyard Street. Neighborhood boundaries: (north) West Greenfield Avenue; (south) West Becher Street; (east) South Fifth Street; (west) South Sixteenth Street. Neighborhood boundaries: (north) West Hampton Avenue; (south) West

Capitol Drive; (east) West Fond Du Lac Avenue; (west) North Seventy-Sixth Street, partial, Wisconsin Highway 175.

29. Neighborhood boundaries: (north) West Capitol Drive; (south) West Keefe Avenue; (east) Highway 43; (west) North Twentieth Street.

30. Neighborhood boundaries: (north) West Seeboth Street, partial, Menomonee River; (south) West Greenfield Avenue; (east) South First Street; (west) South Cesar Chavez Drive/South Sixteenth Street.

31. Also known as Kilbourn Town. Neighborhood boundaries: (north) West McKinley Avenue; (south) I-794 East; (east) Milwaukee River; (west) I-43.

32. Neighborhood boundaries: (north) North Pleasant Street; (south) West McKinley Avenue; (east) Milwaukee River; (west) Dr. Martin Luther King Jr. Drive.

33. Also known as Juneau Town. Neighborhood boundaries: (north) East Ogden Avenue, partial, East State Street; (south) East Clybourn Street; (east) Lincoln Memorial Drive; (west) Milwaukee River.

34. Neighborhood boundaries: (north) West Highland Boulevard; (south) West Wisconsin Avenue; (east) North Thirty-Fifth Street; (west) Wisconsin Highway 175.

35. Neighborhood boundaries: (north) Hank Aaron State Trail; (south) West Greenfield Avenue; (east) South Layton Boulevard; (west) South Thirty-First Street.

36. Neighborhood boundaries: (north) I-94, partial, I-794; (south) Hank Aaron State Trail, partial, Menomonee River, partial; (east) Milwaukee River; (west) Miller Park Way.

37. Neighborhood boundaries: (north) West Seeboth Street, partial, Menomonee River; (south) West Greenfield Avenue; (east) South First Street; (west) South Cesar Chavez Drive/South Sixteenth Street.

38. Neighborhood boundaries: (north) West Highland Boulevard; (south) West Wisconsin Avenue; (east) North Twenty-Seventh Street; (west) North Thirty-Fifth Street.

39. Neighborhood boundaries: (north) KK River Trail; (south) Kinnickinnick River; (east) Kinnickinnick River; (west) South First Street/South Kinnickinnick Avenue.

40. Neighborhood boundaries: (north) West Seeboth Street, partial, Menomonee River; (south) West Greenfield Avenue; (east) South First Street; (west) South Cesar Chavez Drive/South Sixteenth Street.

41. Neighborhood boundaries: (north) Commerce Street; (south) Pleasant Street; (east) North Riverwalk Way; (west) North Hubbard Street, partial.

42. Neighborhood boundaries: (north) Milwaukee River; (south) East Pearson Street; (east) North Humboldt Avenue; (west) Milwaukee River.

43. Neighborhood boundaries: (north) East Capitol Drive; (south) Milwaukee River; (east) Milwaukee River; (west) North Holton Street.

44. Also known as Kilbourn Town. Neighborhood boundaries: (north) West McKinley Avenue; (south) I-794 East; (east) Milwaukee River; (west) I-43.

45. Also known as Kilbourn Town. Neighborhood boundaries: (north) West McKinley Avenue; (south) I-794 East; (east) Milwaukee River; (west) I-43.

46. Neighborhood boundaries: (north) East North Avenue; (south) East Ogden Avenue; (east) North Prospect Avenue; (west) North Humboldt Avenue, partial, Milwaukee River.

Part 4

47. Also known as Juneau Town. Neighborhood boundaries: (north) East Ogden Avenue, partial, East State Street; (south) East Clybourn Street; (east) Lincoln Memorial Drive; (west) Milwaukee River.

48. Neighborhood boundaries: (north) East Oklahoma Avenue; (south) East St. Francis Avenue, partial; (east) Lake Michigan; (west) Lake Parkway-794.

49. Neighborhood boundaries: (north) West Concordia Avenue; (south) West Center Street; (east) North Eighty-Ninth Street; (west) Menomonee River Parkway.

50. Neighborhood boundaries: (north) West Ohio Avenue; (south) West Morgan Avenue; (east) South Thirty-Fifth Street; (west) South Thirty-Ninth Street.

51. Also called Kilbourn Town. Neighborhood boundaries: (north) West McKinley Avenue; (south) I-794 East; (east) Milwaukee River; (west) I-43.

52. Neighborhood boundaries: (north) West Highland Boulevard; (south) West Wisconsin Avenue; (east) North Twenty-Seventh Street; (west) North Thirty-Fifth Street.

53. Also known as Juneau Town. Neighborhood boundaries: (north) East Ogden Avenue, partial, East State Street; (south) East Clybourn Street; (east) Lincoln Memorial Drive; (west) Milwaukee River.

54. Neighborhood boundaries: (north) West Highland Avenue; (south) West Clybourn Avenue, partial, I-94–West Kilbourn Avenue; (east) North Eleventh Street, partial, North Twenty-First Street; (west) North Twenty-Seventh Street.

55. Neighborhood boundaries: (north) West Burleigh Street; (south) West Center Street; (east) North Forty-Third Street; (west) North Sixtieth Street.

56. Neighborhood boundaries: (north) West Silver Spring Drive; (south) West Cornell Street; (east) North Green Bay Avenue; (west) North Teutonia Avenue.

Part 5

57. Neighborhood boundaries: (north) North Lincoln Memorial Drive; (south) North Lincoln Memorial Drive; (east) Lake Michigan; (west) North Lake Drive, partial.
58. Neighborhood boundaries: (north) North Halyard Street; (south) West Fond du Lac Avenue; (east) North Sixth Street; (west) Highway 43.
59. Neighborhood boundaries: (north) West Seeboth Street, partial, Menomonee River; (south) West Greenfield Avenue; (east) South First Street; (west) South Cesar Chavez Drive/South Sixteenth Street.
60. Neighborhood boundaries: (north) West Keefe Avenue; (south) West North Avenue; (east) North Holton Street; (west) Highway 43.
61. Neighborhood boundaries: (north) West Vliet Street; (south) West Highland Boulevard; (east) North Twenty-Seventh Street; (west) North Thirty-Fifth Street.
62. Also called Juneau Town. Neighborhood boundaries: (north) East Ogden Avenue, partial, East State Street; (south) East Clybourn Street; (east) Lincoln Memorial Drive; (west) Milwaukee River.
63. Neighborhood boundaries: (north) West Calumet, partial; (south) West Good Hope Avenue; (east) Union Pacific Railroad Company; (west) North Seventy-Sixth Street.
64. Neighborhood boundaries: (north) East Locust Street; (south) East North Avenue; (east) North Downer Avenue; (west) North Oakland Avenue.
65. Also known as Kilbourn Town. Neighborhood boundaries: (north) West McKinley Avenue; (south) I-794 East; (east) Milwaukee River; (west) I-43.
66. Neighborhood boundaries: (north) East North Avenue; (south) East Ogden Avenue; (east) North Prospect Avenue; (west) North Humboldt Avenue, partial, Milwaukee River.
67. Neighborhood boundaries: (north) West North Avenue; (south) West Vliet Street; (east) North Thirty-Fifth Street; (west) North Forty-Seventh Street.
68. Neighborhood location: (north) West Roosevelt Drive, partial; (south) West Capitol Drive; (east) North Teutonia Avenue; (west) North Thirtieth Street, partial.

Part 6

69. Neighborhood boundaries: (north) West Becher Street; (south) West Harrison Avenue; (east) I-94 Freeway; (west) South Sixteenth Street.

70. Halyard Park boundaries: (north) West North Avenue; (south) West Walnut Street; (east) Dr. Martin Luther King Jr. Drive; (west) North Halyard Street. Brewer's Hill boundaries: (north) West North Avenue; (south) West Walnut Street; (east) North Holton Street; (west) Dr. Martin Luther King Jr. Drive.

71. Neighborhood boundaries: (north) West Highland Avenue; (south) West Clybourn Avenue, partial, I-94–West Kilbourn Avenue; (east) North Eleventh Street, partial, North Twenty-First Street; (west) North Twenty-Seventh Street.

72. Neighborhood boundaries: (north) West Vliet Street; (south) West Highland Boulevard; (east) North Twenty-Seventh Street; (west) North Thirty-Fifth Street.

73. Neighborhood boundaries: (north) West Walnut Street; (south) West Highland Avenue; (east) Highway 43; (west) North Twentieth Street, partial.

74. Neighborhood boundaries: (north) West Hampton Avenue; (south) West Congress Street; (east) North Sherman Boulevard; (west) West Parkway Drive.

75. Neighborhood boundaries: (north) Railroad tracks; (south) West Pierce Street; (east) North Sixteenth Street; (west) South Layton Boulevard.

76. Neighborhood boundaries: (north) West Good Hope; (south) Union Pacific Railroad Company; (east) West Sixtieth Street; (west) North Seventy-Sixth Street.

77. Neighborhood boundaries: (north) East Clybourn Street; (south) East Erie Street; (east) Lake Michigan; (west) Milwaukee River.

78. Neighborhood boundaries: (north) East Clybourn Street; (south) East Erie Street; (east) Lake Michigan; (west) Milwaukee River.

79. Halyard Park boundaries: (north) West North Avenue; (south) West Walnut Street; (east) Dr. Martin Luther King Jr. Drive; (west) North Halyard Street. Hillside boundaries: (north) North Halyard Street; (south) West Fond du Lac Avenue; (east) North Sixth Street; (west) Highway 43. Haymarket boundaries: (north) West Walnut Street; (south) West McKinley Avenue; (east) Dr. Martin Luther King Jr. Drive; (west) North Sixth Street. Triangle North: (north) West North Avenue; (south) West Fond Du Lac Avenue; (east) Highway 43; (west) West Fond du Lac Avenue.

Part 7

80. Also known as Kilbourn Town. Neighborhood boundaries: (north) West McKinley Avenue; (south) I-794 East; (east) Milwaukee River; (west) I-43.

81. Neighborhood boundaries: (north) West Kilbourn; (south) West Clybourn; (east) I-43; (west) North Twenty-First Street.

82. Also known as Juneau Town. Neighborhood boundaries: (north) East Ogden Avenue, partial, East State Street; (south) East Clybourn Street; (east) Lincoln Memorial Drive; (west) Milwaukee River.
83. Neighborhood boundaries: (north) railroad; (south) West Silver Spring Drive; (east) North Sherman Boulevard; (west) North Sixtieth Street.

Part 8

84. Also called Kilbourn Town. Neighborhood boundaries: (north) West McKinley Avenue; (south) I-794 East; (east) Milwaukee River; (west) I-43.
85. Yankee Hill neighborhood boundaries: (north) East Ogden Avenue; (south) East State Street; (east) North Lincoln Memorial Drive; (west) North Jackson Street. Cooper Park boundaries: (north) West Burleigh Street; (south) West Center Street; (east) North Seventy-Sixth Street; (west) North Eighty-Ninth Street. Washington Park boundaries: (north) West North Avenue; (south) West Vliet Street; (east) North Thirty-Fifth Street; (west) North Forty-Seventh Street. Lake Park boundaries: (north) North Lincoln Memorial Drive; (south) North Lincoln Memorial Drive; (east) Lake Michigan; (west) North Lake Drive, partial.
86. Neighborhood boundaries: (north) Kinnickinnick River; (south) East Morgan Avenue; (east) Lake Michigan; (west) I-94.

Bibliography

Part 1: Remains of Earliest German Settlements in Milwaukee Neighborhoods

Ancestry. "United States Census, Milwaukee, Milwaukee County." www.ancestry.com.

———. "U.S. City Directories, 1822–1995." www.ancestry.com.

———. "U.S. Civil War Soldiers." www.ancestry.com.

———. "U.S. Find a Grave Index, 1600s to Current." www.ancestry.com.

Arends, Shirley Fischer. *The Central Dakota Germans: Their History, Language and Culture.* Nacogdoches, TX: SFA Publishing, 2016.

Bird, Miriam Y. *A History of Granville Township.* N.p: Self-published, 1996.

Gurda, John. *The Making of Milwaukee.* Milwaukee, WI: Milwaukee County Historical Society, 1999.

———. *Milwaukee, City of Neighborhoods.* Milwaukee, WI: Historic Milwaukee Inc., 2015.

———. *One People, Many Paths: A History of Jewish Milwaukee.* Milwaukee, WI: Jewish Museum Milwaukee, 2009.

Jewish Museum Milwaukee. "Milwaukee Jewish Timeline." www.jewishmuseummilwaukee.org.

Jones, Catherine R., Patricia B. Richards, Christina L. Zweig and Eric E. Burant. *Archaeological and Osteological Analysis of Burials Recovered from the Second Ward Cemetery (47MI0523).* Milwaukee: University of Wisconsin–Milwaukee Cultural Resource Management, 2018.

Kriehn, Ruth. *The Fisherfolk of Jones Island*. Milwaukee, WI: Milwaukee County Historical Society, 1988.

Lackey, Jill F. *Ethnic Practices in the Twenty-First Century: The Milwaukee Study*. Latham, MD: Lexington Press, 2013.

Lackey, Jill F., and Rick Petrie. *Strolling through Milwaukee's Ethnic History*. Milwaukee, WI: MECAH Publishing, 2013.

Milwaukee Journal. "Old Town Lives on Their Memories." May 5, 1976.

———. "The Other Fellow's Job." June 23, 1947.

———. "People of the River." July 8, 1981.

———. "Sure Milwaukee Has Strong German Roots, But What Does That Heritage Mean Today?" June 24, 1990.

———. "World Ignored Postwar Persecution." July 8, 1981.

Milwaukee Sentinel. "Granville." March 22, 1877.

Sallet, Richard. *Russian-German Settlement in the United States*. Fargo: North Dakota Institute for Regional Studies, 1974.

Tolzmann, Don Heinrich. *The German American Experience*. Amherst, NY: Humanity Books, 2000.

Urban Anthropology Inc. "191 Milwaukee Neighborhoods." www.neighborhoodsinmilwaukee.org.

———. *The People Nobody Knew: The Kaszubs of Jones Island*. Milwaukee, WI: Urban Anthropology Inc., 2004.

Watson Schumacher, Jennifer, ed. *German Milwaukee*. Charleston, SC: Arcadia Publishing, 2009.

Part 2: German Place Names in Milwaukee Neighborhoods

Albano, Laurie Muench. *Milwaukee County Parks*. Charleston, SC: Arcadia Publishing, 2007.

Ancestry. "Milwaukee, Wisconsin Directory, 1889–1890." www.ancestry.com.

———. "Milwaukee, Wisconsin, Marriages, 1838–1911." www.ancestry.com.

———. "United States Census, Milwaukee, Milwaukee County." www.ancestry.com.

———. "U.S. City Directories, 1822–1995." www.ancestry.com.

———. "U.S. Find a Grave Index, 1600s to Current." www.ancestry.com.

———. "Wisconsin, Births and Christenings Index, 1801–1928." www.ancestry.com.

Baehr, Carl. *Milwaukee Streets: The Stories Behind Their Names*. Milwaukee, WI: Cream City Press, 1995.

Gurda, John. *The Making of Milwaukee*. Milwaukee, WI: Milwaukee County Historical Society, 1999.

———. *Milwaukee, City of Neighborhoods*. Milwaukee, WI: Historic Milwaukee Inc., 2015.

Milwaukee Sentinel. "Wolf Hunting in the Suburbs." January 25, 1876.

Urban Anthropology Inc. "191 Milwaukee Neighborhoods." www. neighborhoodsinmilwaukee.org.

Part 3: Remains of German Commerce in Milwaukee Neighborhoods

Ancestry. "United States Census, Milwaukee, Milwaukee County." www. ancestry.com.

———. "U.S. City Directories, 1822–1995." www.ancestry.com.

———. "U.S. Find a Grave Index, 1600s to Current." www.ancestry.com.

Brooke, Zach. "Murder of a Tyrant." *Milwaukee Magazine,* May 29, 2015. www. milwaukeemag.com.

Buetner, Jeff. "Gimbel's Department Store, 1925." *Urban Milwaukee,* April 18, 2018. www.urbanmilwaukee.com.

Geenen, Paul. *Schuster's and Gimbels: Milwaukee's Beloved Department Stores.* Charleston, SC: The History Press, 2012.

Gurda, John. *Cream City Chronicles: Stories of Milwaukee's Past.* Madison: Wisconsin Historical Society Press, 2007.

———. *The Making of "A Good Name in Industry."* Milwaukee, WI: Falk Corporation, 1991.

———. *The Making of Milwaukee.* Milwaukee, WI: Milwaukee County Historical Society, 1999.

Milwaukee Journal. "All Jewish Program." October 25, 1953.

———. "Big Event on Upper Third Street." December 1, 1931.

———. "Calling Val Blatz: Blatz' Ghost a Halloween No-Show." November 1, 1990.

———. "Gallun Ending Tanning Business." January 20, 1993.

———. "Heileman Shuts Brewery Here: Blatz Plant May Have Been Victim of Shift from Specialty Beers." August 10, 1989.

———. "Huge Candle to Light Grocers' Convention." March 26, 1941.

———. "Joe Scriba's Milwaukee." December 31, 1978.

———. "Links to the Past: After 100 Years." March 23, 1980.

———. "Local Business Areas Thriving." December 1, 1932.

————. "Many Former Trostel Workers Able to Find New Employment." July 31, 1969.

————. "Many Offer to Help Find Jobs for Tannery Workers." June 3, 1969.

————. "MSOE Gets Right to Buy Beer Baron's Building." March 27, 1989.

————. "New Life at the Old Brewery: Solid Stock Houses a Harvest of Apartments." July 31, 1988.

————. "Saturday Is Last Day for Beer Baron's." May 18, 1989.

————. "Set Rites for Monday for Mrs. Lina Baench." May 5, 1951.

————. "Trostel, Union Negotiating; Rumors Hint Plant Closing." May 23, 1969.

Milwaukee Journal Sentinel. "The Beer is Going…But the Brewery—." October 18, 1996.

————. "Black Ribbon Day: Taps for Pabst." October 18, 1996.

————. "For Pabst's Patriarch, a Bittersweet Aftertaste." October 10, 1996.

————. "Harnischfeger Plans to Reorganize." October 27, 2000.

————. "Harnischfeger to Sell Most of Its P&H Unit." January 29, 1998.

————. "Journey from N. 3rd St. to King Drive was Not a Smooth Ride." April 2, 2018.

————. "Milwaukee Police: Initial Investigation." March 4, 2020.

————. "Name Game: What's Harnischfeger Worth?" June 30, 2001.

————. "OSHA Metes Out Fines in Falk Blast." May 8, 2007.

————. "Pabst Shutdown a Big Blow to Brew City." October 18, 1996.

————. "Tannery's Recent History Was Marked by Upheaval." February 5, 2000.

————. "This Hurts More Than Usual." February 28, 2020.

————. "Tragedy at Falk Corp: Workers Grieve Lost Lives." December 8, 2006.

————. "U.S. Leather to Close Plant Here, Cut 600 Jobs." February 3, 2000.

————. "What Would Mr. Harnischfeger Make of It?" September 12, 1999.

Milwaukee Sentinel. "Coming! Santa and Me-Tiks." November 13, 1941.

————. "Masonic Burial Friday for Fred Usinger." July 31, 1930.

————. "Promotion for Streets." December 9, 1938.

————. "Rosenberg Is Feted by His Employees [*sic*]." June 22, 1927.

————. "Schuster's 'New Era' 12th and Vliet St. Store." November 5, 1937.

————. "Schuster's New Era 12th & Vliet Street Store." December 2, 1937.

————. "Variety on Third Street." September 19, 1948.

New York Times. "Hire Minorities, US Tells Breweries." December 18, 1970.

————. "Milwaukeeans Face Loss of One of Their Own in Closing Schlitz Brewery." August 9, 1981.

Still, Bayrd. *Milwaukee: The History of a City.* Madison: State Historical Society of Wisconsin, 1948.

Tanzilo, Bobby. "Urban Spelunking: Mader's Restaurant." *OnMilwaukee*, October 29, 2019. www.onmilwaukee.com.

Trotter, Joe William, Jr. *Black Milwaukee: The Making of an Industrial Proletariat 1915–45.* Chicago: University of Illinois Press, 2007.

Urban Anthropology Inc. "191 Milwaukee Neighborhoods." www. neighborhoodsinmilwaukee.org.

Wells, Robert W. *This Is Milwaukee.* Garden City, NY: Doubleday & Co. Inc., 1970.

Part 4: Remains of German Institutions in Milwaukee Neighborhoods

Ancestry. "United States Census, Milwaukee, Milwaukee County." www. ancestry.com.

Ascension Wisconsin. "Ascension Wisconsin—Our Heritage, Our Story." www. ascension.org.

Lackey, Jill F. *Ethnic Practices in the Twenty-First Century: The Milwaukee Study.* Latham, MD: Lexington Press, 2013.

Lackey, Jill F., and Rick Petrie. *Strolling through Milwaukee's Ethnic History.* Milwaukee, WI: MECAH Publishing, 2013.

Milwaukee Journal. "Concordia-Area Residents to Take Their Case to Synod." August 19, 1982.

Still, Bayrd. *Milwaukee: The History of a City.* Madison: State Historical Society of Wisconsin, 1948.

Tanzilo, Bobby. "Urban Spelunking: Another Former Concordia Campus Renovation Update." *OnMilwaukee*, March 8, 2018. www.onmilwaukee.com.

Tolan, Thomas L. *Riverwest: A Community History.* Milwaukee, WI: Past Press, in cooperation with COA Youth & Family Centers, *2003*.

Urban Anthropology Inc. "191 Milwaukee Neighborhoods." www. neighborhoodsinmilwaukee.org.

Part 5: Remains of German Ways of Life in Milwaukee Neighborhoods

Ancestry. "United States Census, Milwaukee, Milwaukee County." www. ancestry.com.

Beck, Elmer. *The Sewer Socialists: A History of the Socialist Party of Wisconsin, 1897–1940.* Fennimore, WI: Westburg Associates, *1982*.

Lackey, Jill Florence, dir. *The Cultural Roots of Milwaukee's Socialist Movement.* Milwaukee, WI: Urban Anthropology Inc., 2007.

Milwaukee Examiner. "The Pabst Theater." April 16, 2009.

Milwaukee Journal. "Among the Wheelmen: Many Entries for the Cold Spring Park-North Side Century Run." July 23, 1896.

———. "The German Gold Coast: Historic Harambee Has Evolved." July 24, 1994.

———. "Johnson Gets Home: The Minneapolis Wheelman Talks About the European Wheel Riders." August 3, 1896.

———. "A Race at Cold Spring Park: Cyclone and Chester Matched Against Each Other for $70 a Side." December 10, 1890.

———. "Remember When…A Pagoda Stood in Schlitz Park?" November 16, 1969.

———. "When the Pabst Was Young and Gay." May 6, 1967.

Milwaukee Journal Sentinel. "Clair Bloom Extends Great Acting Tradition." April 27, 1990.

Milwaukee Sentinel. "Historians to Find Theaters with Strange Second Lives." July 8, 1981.

———. "Milwaukee's Movie Palaces in Spotlight." May 11, 1984.

———. "Pabst Theater Named Historic Landmark." December 11, 1991.

Still, Bayrd. *Milwaukee: The History of a City.* Madison: State Historical Society of Wisconsin, 1948

Urban Anthropology Inc. "191 Milwaukee Neighborhoods." www.neighborhoodsinmilwaukee.org.

Wells, Robert W. *This Is Milwaukee.* Garden City, NY: Doubleday & Co. Inc., 1970.

Part 6: German Footprints on the Physical Terrain in Milwaukee Neighborhoods

Albano, Laurie Muench. *Milwaukee County Parks.* Charleston, SC: Arcadia Publishing, 2007.

Ancestry. "United States Census, Milwaukee, Milwaukee County." www.ancestry.com.

———. "U.S. Naturalization Record Indexes, 1791–1992." www.ancestry.com.

Downing, Willard E. "Lessons for Redevelopers Seen in End of Italian 'Island' Here." *Milwaukee Journal,* August 7, 1960.

Gurda, John. *The Making of Milwaukee.* Milwaukee, WI: Milwaukee County Historical Society, 1999.

Milwaukee Journal. "Artists and Architects Discuss Tavern Styles." April 7, 1933.
————. "Buildings Show Changes in Design." May 20, 1962.
————. "For New Conservatory: Park Board Selects a Site in Mitchell Park." April 11, 1898.
————. "Maier Fires Back at Zeidler Claims." March 21, 1963.
————. "New Summerfest Schedule Set; Variety of Entertainment Certain." May 30, 1968.
————. "Soccer/Kickers Club Agree to Buy Field." May 12, 1991.
————. "A Tradition in Polo for 33 Years." July 19, 1984.
Milwaukee Sentinel. "Development Stumbles on Stalled Projects." March 30, 1972.
————. "Former Residents Keep Walnut St. Memories Alive." May 7, 1995.
————. "Mitchell Park Conservatory Closes Sunday." July 9, 1955.
————. "Trend in Living: An Architectural Legacy." January 2, 1982.
————. "Zeidler Calls Renew Plan Step Backward." October 4, 1962.
Norman, Jack. "Maier Didn't Feel 'Pain' of the City." *Milwaukee Journal,* July 20, 1994.
Olive, Ralph D. "Citizens Organize, Core Area Blooms." *Milwaukee Journal,* December 26, 1968.
Raasch, Nettie L. *From the Cotton Patch to the Inner City.* Milwaukee, WI: N.p., 2004.
Urban Anthropology Inc. "191 Milwaukee Neighborhoods." www.neighborhoodsinmilwaukee.org.
Zeidler, Frank P. *A Liberal in City Government: My Experiences as Mayor of Milwaukee.* Milwaukee, WI: Milwaukee Publishers, 2005.

Part 7: Efforts to Remove German Footprints from Milwaukee Neighborhoods

Gurda, John. *Cream City Chronicles: Stories of Milwaukee's Past.* Madison: Wisconsin Historical Society Press, 2007.
————. *The Making of Milwaukee.* Milwaukee, WI: Milwaukee County Historical Society, 1999.
Jacobson, Brian. "The Mystery of the Germania Statue." *Urban Milwaukee,* August 13, 2013. www.urbanmilwaukee.com.
Milwaukee Journal. "Aide at Bund Camp Is Held." December 15, 1941.
————. "Enemy Aliens to Face Quiz." December 11, 1941.
Milwaukee Sentinel. "Heil Gardener Will Be Held 'For Duration.'" April 23, 1942.
————. "Workhouse Viewed as Concentration Camp: New Arrests." December 14, 1941.

Stevens, John D. "When Dissent Was a Sin in Milwaukee." *Milwaukee Sentinel*, March 10, 1966.

Urban Anthropology Inc. "191 Milwaukee Neighborhoods." www.neighborhoodsinmilwaukee.org.

Wells, Robert W. *This Is Milwaukee*. Garden City, NY: Doubleday & Co. Inc., 1970.

Part 8: Restoring Milwaukee's German Essence

Gurda, John. "Bucks' Deer District Rises." *Milwaukee Journal Sentinel*, October 6, 2019.

Milwaukee Ethnic News. "Christkindlmarket Premiered in 2018 to Large Crowds." January/February 2019.

Milwaukee Neighborhood Forum. "$10 and Under Neighborhood Events." June/July 2019.

"National Register of Historic Places Inventory Nomination Form." Washington DC: United States Department of the Interior, National Park Service. February 9, 1987.

INDEX

A

Adler family 67
Adrian family 48
Alverno College 132, 134, 135, 196
Alverno neighborhood 135
Anneke, Mathilde 41
Annenberg family 36, 37, 153
annexation of Granville 31
Arlington Heights neighborhood 87
Auer family 66
Avenues West neighborhood 140, 165

B

Baensch, Lina "Ma" 116, 117
Baran Park neighborhood 175
Bauer, Alex 153
Bavaria Brewery 102
Bay View neighborhood 69, 201
beer gardens 13, 92, 145, 147, 148, 149, 158, 200, 201
Beerline B neighborhood 111, 113
Bettinger family 67

Billie the Brownie 79
Bitker-Gerner's 77
Blatz 96, 97, 196
Blatz Brewing Company 95, 96, 97, 196
Blatz, Valentin 95, 98
Brachmann, Oscar 153
Brewer's Hill neighborhood 75, 165
Brewhouse Inn & Suites 93
Brielmaier, Erhard 162
Brynwood neighborhood 152
Burleigh Street shopping hub 82, 84

C

Capitol Court 77, 86
Capitol Heights neighborhood 86
Cardinal Stritch 135
Christkindlesmarket 199
Clarke Square neighborhood 67
Clas, Alfred C. 155
Cold Spring Park neighborhood 79, 149, 150, 167
Cold Spring Racing Course 150

Concordia University 136
Congregation Emanu-El B'ne
    Jeshurun 34, 38
Cooper Park neighborhood 200
Cultural Resource Management of
    the University of Wisconsin-
    Milwaukee 19

D

Deaconess Hospital 140, 196
Deuster family 23, 24
Deutscher Club 187
Dick, Gustave A. 153, 165
Donauschwaben 54, 55, 56, 58

E

East Town neighborhood 95, 128,
    137, 189

F

Fair Park neighborhood 70
Falk Corporation 102, 103, 104, 196
Falk explosion 104
Falk, Franz 102
Fernwood neighborhood 130
Forty-Eighters 39, 41, 187, 198
freeway disruption 81, 84, 174, 177,
    178, 196
Freis, Adam 63
Freistadt 17, 21

G

Gallun, August Friedrich 114
Gallun Tannery 114
Garden District 61
Garden Homes neighborhood 158, 196
German Athens 12, 13, 151, 152,
    185, 195, 198, 200

German-English Academy 37,
    138, 187
Germania building 163, 185, 198
German internment 191
German Jews 33, 36
German Russian healers 53
Germans from Russia in Old North
    Milwaukee 50
Gimbel, Adam 86
Gimbels Department Store 85
Goethe-Schiller monument 155, 196
Grace Lutheran Congregational
    Church 51
Granville Township 27, 30, 32, 50,
    171, 191
Grasslyn Manor neighborhood 82
Great Depression 64, 76, 83, 88, 99,
    105, 106, 113, 116, 118
Gruenhagen brothers 18

H

Halyard Park neighborhood 86,
    165, 178
Harambee neighborhood 75, 149
Harbor View neighborhood 107
Harnischfeger Corporation 104,
    105, 106
Harnischfeger, Henry 105
Havenwoods neighborhood 191
Haymarket neighborhood 178
Henni, John Martin 129
Henry Maier Festival Park 172
Hillside neighborhood 147, 178
Historic Concordia neighborhood
    105, 136
Historic Mitchell neighborhood 86
Historic Third Ward neighborhood
    34, 172, 175, 178
Hoffmann, Charles G. 165
House of Correction 191

J

Johnson's Woods neighborhood 67
Jones Island neighborhood 43, 46,
    47, 48, 49
Joseph Schlitz Brewing Company 93,
    94, 147, 171, 196
Joy Global Inc. 107

K

King Park neighborhood 17, 79, 167
Kirchoff, Charles 153
Koch, Henry C. 162
Kriehn family 47
Krug, August 93

L

Lake Park neighborhood 155
Landmark 1850 Inn 62
Leidersdorf, Bernhard 68
Lincoln Park neighborhood 141
Lincoln Village neighborhood 163,
    165, 175
Lotharius, Karl Heinz 122, 124
Lower East Side neighborhood 121,
    124, 154
Lueddemann's-on-the-Lake 145,
    146, 201
Lutheran Hospital 139, 140

M

Ma Baensch's herring 116, 196
Machek House 167
Mack Acres neighborhood 64
Mack, Rudolph 64
Mader family 119, 121
Mader's Restaurant 119, 196, 199
Maier, Henry 78, 172, 174, 180, 196
Maple Tree neighborhood 28, 31

Marquette neighborhood 187
Martin Drive neighborhood 79
Meinecke family 65
Menomonee River Hills East
    neighborhood 171
Menomonee Valley neighborhood 103
Merrill Park neighborhood 175
Messmer High School 132
Midtown neighborhood 56, 79
Militzer, Herman 79
Militzer Quick Service 79
Miller Brewing Company 97, 98, 99
Miller, Frederick 98
Miller Park 99, 206
Miller Valley neighborhood 99
Milwaukee Polo Field 171
Milwaukee School of Engineering
    97, 137, 196
Milwaukee's Socialists 157
Mitchell Park Horticultural
    Conservatory 169, 170
Mitchell Park neighborhood 170
Molson Coors Beverage Company
    97, 100
Mount Mary 132, 134, 196
Mount Mary neighborhood 134

N

National Park neighborhood 102
New Coeln House 62
New Coeln neighborhood 22, 61
North Division neighborhood 65
Northpoint neighborhood 69
Nunnemacher's Grand Opera
    House 152

O

Old Lutherans 17
Old North Milwaukee
    neighborhood 50

Old World Third Street 78, 117, 198
Oriental Theater 37, 121, 153
Otto, William Ferdinand 18

P

Pabst Brewery 90, 92, 102, 135,
    165, 196
Pabst, Frederick 90, 102, 149, 152
Pabst Theater 103, 152, 165, 185, 198
Park View neighborhood 79
Pawling and Harnischfeger 105
Pennsylvania Dutch 27
Pfister and Vogel 108, 109
Pfister, Guido 108
Pfister Hotel 110, 111, 163
Phillip Best Brewery 90
Pigsville neighborhood 63
Plank Road Brewery 99
Pomeranian Germans of Jones
    Island 44
Prohibition 91, 94, 96, 99, 120, 148,
    149, 158, 200

R

racial issues 94, 106, 197
Red Town 53
Reuthlisberger, Herman 89
Rieder's 121, 122, 123
Rietschel, Ernst Friedrich August 155
River House apartments 115
River Place Lofts Condominiums 111
Riverwest neighborhood 66, 75, 117,
    129, 165
Roosevelt Grove neighborhood 82
Rosenberg's Fine Apparel 76

S

Salem Lutheran Church 28
Salem Lutheran Landmark Church 29

Salm Naegele, Anna 55
Scheftels Herbst, Emma 33
Schlinger brothers 70
Schlitz beer gardens
    Palm Garden 147
    Schlitz Park 147
    Trivoli Palm Garden 147
Schlitz, Joseph 93
Schlitz Office Park 95
Schlitz Park neighborhood 93
Schnetzky, Herman Paul 163
School Sisters of Notre Dame 132,
    134, 136
School Sisters of St. Francis 134
Schuetzen Park 149
Schulte, Victor 129, 130
Schuster, Edward 76
Schuster's Christmas Parade 79
Schuster's Department Store 76, 79
Schwister family 31
Second Ward Cemetery 18, 19
Sherman Park area 38, 82, 83, 141
Sherman Park neighborhood 82
Sherman Theater 84
Sieker, Johann Heinrich 30
Sisters of St. Francis of Assisi 135
Steinhafel family 88
Steinhafel's Furniture 87
St. Francis de Sales Seminary 129,
    130, 131
St. Joseph Hospital 140, 141
St. Joseph neighborhood 82, 141
St. Mary Parish 128
St. Michael Hospital 141
St. Michael Parish 56
Strack, Otto 152, 163
St. Stephen's Catholic Church 22,
    23, 24
Sunset Heights neighborhood 82

T

Triangle North neighborhood 178
Trostel, Albert Gottlieb 111
Trostel Square Apartments 113, 196
Trostel Tannery 111, 196
Turner Hall 40, 41, 42, 162, 198
Turners 39, 40, 41, 162, 187, 190

U

Uihlein family 93, 94, 171
Uihlein Soccer Park 94, 172
University School of Milwaukee 37, 39
Upper East Side neighborhood 34, 36, 38
Upper Third Street 75, 76, 86
Uptown neighborhood 82
urban renewal 129, 174, 176, 178, 180, 196
Usinger family 117, 118
Usinger's Sausage 117, 118, 199

V

Vliet Street shopping hub 78
Vogel, Frederick 108
Von Trier 121, 122, 123, 124, 196

W

Wahl, Christian 69, 146, 169, 170
Wahl Park neighborhood 70, 169
Walker's Point neighborhood 89, 108, 119, 147
Walnut Improvement Council 180
Wambold, Samuel 28
Washington Park neighborhood 79, 155, 200
Washington Park Zoo 79, 80
Wenz, Arthur 69
Werwath, Oscar 137

Westown neighborhood 17, 40, 90, 117, 120, 135, 154, 185, 187, 198, 199, 200
Wilson Park neighborhood 106
Wisconsin Club 187
Wisconsin Synod, founding 28
World War I 54, 64, 105, 109, 148, 185, 186, 189
World War II 30, 54, 55, 56, 58, 64, 76, 88, 103, 105, 109, 113, 118, 120, 138, 190, 191

Y

Yankee Hill neighborhood 37, 129, 200

Z

Zeidler, Frank 174, 176, 180, 196
Zilber, Joseph A. 92
Zirgibel family 51, 52

ABOUT THE AUTHORS

Both Jill Florence Lackey and Rick Petrie are longtime residents of Milwaukee, Wisconsin.

Dr. Lackey, having taught anthropology at Marquette University for twelve years, was the founder of Urban Anthropology Inc., where she continues to serve as the principal investigator in charge of research. Having earned a doctorate in urban cultural anthropology, she is the author of thirteen books, including *Ethnic Practices in the Twenty-First Century: The Milwaukee Study, Strolling through Milwaukee's Ethnic History* and *Milwaukee's Old South Side*.

Rick Petrie is the executive director of Urban Anthropology Inc. He has a certificate degree in applied anthropology, a bachelor's degree in art from the University of Wisconsin–Milwaukee and has worked as part of the administrative staff for a variety of Milwaukee museums, including the Charles Allis Museum, Villa Terrace Decorative Arts Museum and the Old South Side Settlement Museum. He currently is on the staff of the Milwaukee County Historical Society and is the coauthor of *Strolling through Milwaukee's Ethnic History*.